DECK PLANS

*Created and designed
by the editorial staff of
ORTHO Books*

*Writer and Plan
Designer*
Robert J. Beckstrom

Graphic Designers
Neil Shakery
Sandy McHenry

Illustrator
Rik Olson

Ortho Books

Publisher
Robert L. Iacopi

Editorial Director
Min S. Yee

Managing Editors
Anne Coolman
Michael D. Smith
Sally W. Smith

Production Manager
Ernie S. Tasaki

Editors
Jim Beley
Susan Lammers
Deni Stein

System Manager
Christopher Banks

System Consultant
Mark Zielinski

Asst. System Managers
Linda Bouchard
William F. Yusavage

Photographic Director
Alan Copeland

Photographers
Laurie A. Black
Richard A. Christman

Asst. Production Manager
Darcie S. Furlan

Associate Editors
Richard H. Bond
Alice E. Mace

Production Editors
Don Mosley
Kate O'Keeffe

Chief Copy Editor
Rebecca Pepper

Photo Editors
Anne Pederson
Pam Peirce

National Sales Manager
Garry P. Wellman

Sales Associate
Susan B. Boyle

Operations Director
William T. Pletcher

Operations Assistant
Gail L. Davis

Administrative Assistant
Georgiann Wright

Address all inquiries to
Ortho Books
Chevron Chemical
Company
Consumer Products Division
575 Market Street
San Francisco, CA 94105

Copyright © 1985
Chevron Chemical Company
All rights reserved under
international and Pan-American
copyright conventions.

First Printing in March, 1985

6 7 8 9
87 88 89 90

ISBN 0-89721-043-3 UPC 05921

Library of Congress Catalog Card
Number 85-060006

Acknowledgments

Technical Consultants

Jerry Craig
Southern Forest Products Association
New Orleans, LA

John Reed
Berkeley, CA

Mike Westphal
National Forest Products Association
Columbus, OH

Deck Design Consultants

Randall Fleming
Oakland, CA

Diane C. Snow
Walnut Creek, CA

Deck Designers

Ken Butler, Crescent City, CA: p. 13
Lin Cotton, ASLA, Crystal Lake, CA:
    pp. 4–5, 64–69, 76–77
Phil Decker, Santee, CA: p. 12
Fisher, Wallin, Long Architects, Portland, OR:
    pp. 6–7
George W. Girvin, Royston, Hanamoto, Alley &
    Abbey, Mill Valley, CA: p. 1
Chris E. Hecht, Oakland, CA & Michael Caplan,
    M.D., San Francisco, CA: p. 11 Top
Glen Jarvis, Berkeley, CA: p. 10
Richard K. O'Grady, San Clemente, CA: pp. 18–19
Artemio Paz, Eugene, OR: p. 9
Tatterffield Associates, Vancouver, BC, Canada:
    pp. 16–17
Chris Woerner, Stony Creek, CT: p. 11 (bottom)

Photographers

Laurie Black: p. 1
Ernest Braun/California Redwood Association:
    pp. 76–77
Richard Christman: pp. 8, 10, 11 (top)
John Fulker: pp. 6–7, 9, 16, 16–17
Henson-Hathaway Photographers: Front Cover
    (Cover stylist: Abby Minot)
Balthazar Korab/California Redwood Association:
    pp. 18–19
Fred Lyon: pp. 4–5
Robert Perron/California Redwood Association:
    p. 11 Bottom
Ezra Stoller/ © Esto Photographic Inc.: pp. 14, 15
David H. Swanlund/California Redwood
    Association: p. 13
Wes Thompson/California Redwood Association:
    p. 12

Chevron Chemical Company
575 Market Street, San Francisco, CA 94105

Front Cover:

Plan drawings make a deck possible, including the deck featured on Ortho's best-selling *Decks & Patios* (plans begin on page 64).

Back Cover:

Full-color plan drawings show you everything from a complete rendering of the featured deck to individual details.

Special Thanks to:

Michael Caplan, M.D.
Charlene Draheim
Dan Fuller
Peter Golze
Michael Hamman
Tom Hearne
Chris E. Hecht
Tom Hise
Julian Hodges
Glen Jarvis
Glen Kitzenberger
Bob Lombardi
Michael & Jeanette Lopez
Malcom MacLeod
Robert Malone
Harold Murphrees
National Plan Service
  Elmhurst, IL
Bill Roberts
Chuck Rumwell
Rick Spencer
Petal & Everett Turner
Bill Welte
Paul Winans

DECK PLANS

Choosing a Deck Plan 5
This photographic gallery illustrates six design principles that will help you select a deck plan just right for your home.

Deck Details 77
The Deck Surface 78
Railings 80
Benches 84
Stairs and Steps 86
Deck Finishes 88

Appendix 90
How to Adapt a Deck Plan 90
Deck Terms 94
Index 95
Metric Chart 96

Twelve Deck Plans 19

CHOOSING A DECK PLAN

The following 12 pages illustrate deck design principles that will help you select a deck plan from this book. Use these principles as broad guidelines to help you achieve the goal of a satisfying and successful deck. You will notice that the location of a deck and the amenities added to it (such as benches, furniture, plants, and screens) contribute as much to the deck's impact as the design itself.

The process of selecting a deck plan, deciding on a site, and choosing appropriate amenities should take advantage of all the unique features of your home and site, as well as family needs and aesthetic preferences. The design principles illustrated in this chapter will help you focus on these issues.

It is possible to design a custom deck completely from scratch using these basic principles, or to adapt a plan from this book to suit your needs. The important thing is to be clear about how you intend to use your deck and to survey the site carefully to know what features you want to take advantage of or limitations you need to overcome. A good deck plan grows out of the existing conditions and does not feel like it is imposed on the site.

How to Adapt a Deck Plan. Whatever deck plan you select, you may have to adapt it to fit your specific situation. For guidelines on how to do this, see page 90.

The deck in this photograph illustrates how railings, stairs, furniture, decking patterns, and the site all work together to create a unified whole. It is a deck that serves its functions well and delights the senses. The plans for this deck begin on page 64.

Design Guidelines

A deck should offer privacy and a sense of enclosure. A space that provides seclusion and feels secure is a comfortable place to be. You can design for privacy by locating the deck where it uses existing fences, trees, house walls, or other visual barriers, or by placing screens or fast-growing plants where they are needed. The height of the deck is also critical for privacy. Because most fences are only six feet high, a deck 30 inches off the ground may suddenly put you "on stage" for neighbors and passers-by. One solution to this problem is to use a multilevel deck that has platforms low enough for privacy and high enough for access to the house.

Because distance creates privacy, a deck surrounded by a large expanse of lawn or other landscaping may not need tall screening, but it should have low benches, plants, or other amenities to soften its edges and create a feeling of enclosure.

Surrounded by trees and the house, this deck has privacy on three sides. The tall trees in front of the deck frame the view, making the vista even more dramatic and adding to a sense of security for the viewer. Where the deck extends out over the sloping terrain there is a stairway and railing. They make the edge of the deck safe and inviting. The low benches also create safety barriers and define the activity spaces. All of these features combine to make the deck an inviting and pleasant place to be.

Design Guidelines

A deck's size should be appropriate for its intended uses and available space. As a general rule, decks should be the same size or slightly larger than indoor rooms with the same function. A deck intended for dining should be dining-room size, and one for outdoor congregating should be family-room size, allowing for the fact that most outdoor furniture is slightly larger than indoor.

If your deck will serve more than one purpose, as most decks do, it is best to have distinct areas for each activity. They can be separated by a change in levels, segregated by the deck's shape (an L or T shape, for instance), or defined by amenities like planters or overhead trellises. Each space should still feel generous enough that you don't feel you are being crowded off the deck. Include additional space for circulation and traffic flow.

Overall, the deck should be in proportion with the rest of the house and garden, neither overwhelming nor being dwarfed by them. Local code requirements, such as setback limits and lot-coverage restrictions, may also influence its size.

Right, above and below:
Designed for outdoor dining
and entertaining, this deck
uses a tree planter to define
and separate activity areas
while maintaining a
woodsy feeling.

Far Right: *This deck*
includes ample space for
traffic in and out of the
house, but is still at an
appropriate scale for intimate
conversation or larger group
activities.

Design Guidelines

A deck should be accessible and inviting. People won't use a deck that is hard to get to. If it is attached to the house, it should be accessible from your home's public spaces, such as the kitchen, family room, hallway, dining room, or living room. Decks intended for dining should be close to the kitchen. Ideally, the deck should have two or three entrances from different rooms.

The doorway itself should be wide enough to encourage flow between the indoor and outdoor spaces. French doors, atrium doors, or sliding glass doors (with approved safety glass) add to a deck's appeal and to a sense of continuity between indoors and outdoors. If the deck is not at the same level as the floor of the house, provide a transitional platform so you can go through the doorway without having to step down. The platform should be large enough not to become a bottleneck.

The transition between deck and garden should also be inviting. Make steps wide and graceful. Provide an appealing pathway that meanders toward the deck to create anticipation. Install lighting for nighttime access.

Far left and above: *Wide doorways create an inviting transition between the house and deck, making the deck actually feel like part of the room. Glass doors maintain this feeling even when they are closed. Plants and furniture groupings also create a feeling of transition between the spaces.*

Below: *A dramatic and inviting set of stairs takes you right to the water's edge. Even if your deck site does not have a private lake, you can enhance the deck's beauty and appeal by making steps wider and more luxurious than indoor stairs.*

Design Guidelines

A deck should be comfortable and pleasant. A thoughtful deck is designed for comfort, taking advantage of a yard's individual microclimates. The direction of wind, path of the sun, patterns of shade, and pockets of chilly air are all factors to take into account in locating your deck, choosing its shape and size, and adding amenities.

If you want your deck to be in the sun during certain times of the day or in certain seasons, and out of the sun during others, you can achieve this by taking advantage of shade provided by the house or fences, by annual changes in deciduous trees, or by angles and wraparounds in the deck itself.

You may want to locate the deck where it captures pleasant breezes, or shield it from unwelcome winds, depending on the prevailing climate.

You may find that a high deck gets too much wind, but that a low deck will sit in a basin that traps chilly air at night. You can control these conditions to some extent by choosing your deck site carefully, but you can also choose the deck's size and shape to take advantage of subtle microclimates, or you can design shading structures or windscreens to temper weather conditions.

Views, sounds, and fragrances also contribute to the comfort and sense of delight a deck can provide. Orient the deck toward pleasing views and sounds, mask it from unpleasant ones (freeway or street noise, for instance), and use plants with fragrant blossoms near the deck.

Above: A tall fence provides a windscreen, a sound barrier, and privacy, creating an intimate setting in the middle of a suburban backyard. The deck itself is situated to take advantage of the sun's path, so that the shade from the house provides cool and comfortable areas in the afternoon.

Right: This deck, situated in a heavily wooded region, extends out into a clearing to capture the sunshine. Some of the deck's areas are shaded, offering a choice of sun or shade to suit individual preferences. The deck takes advantage of views and a sense of openness to make it appealing.

Design Guidelines

Left and above: With the deck shown on these two pages, simplicity is the theme on every level. The massive beams, sandy color, and open railings blend beautifully with the rugged and open setting. The site itself imposes no limitations on the deck's size, but its room-sized dimensions help give a human scale to the vast context. When a deck harmonizes with its setting, there is the feeling that it is "just right."

A deck should harmonize with its setting. Imagine your deck as a sculpture to be viewed from many angles, including from below, from above, and from various places on the deck itself. From each viewpoint the deck should blend in with the character of the house or garden to create a unified effect.

If you find it difficult to visualize a given deck plan in your setting, it may help to consider each visual property alone: shape, line, color, texture, and mass.

Your deck's shape should reflect the existing forms in its surroundings. Usually they are rectangles, but angled property lines, curved lawns or swimming pools, and the shape created by the site itself may suggest variations. Generally, simple shapes produce a stronger design than complex shapes.

The edges of the deck, and its railings, are very distinct lines. They should align with strong visual points, such as corners of the house, view

corridors, or forms in the landscape like lawns and planting beds.

Painting or staining a deck is a good way to help it blend in with the house. Another element that reinforces continuity is texture, both of specific materials and of the deck as a whole. Wood is a material that naturally fits in with any garden and most house exteriors, but other materials like stucco, wood siding, wire fencing, and glass can be worked into a deck's railing design to tie it more closely to the house.

A deck's overall sense of mass or form is created by a combination of its height, railings, understructure, and proportions. A deck that is close to the ground can easily blend in with its surroundings, but higher decks should harmonize with the dominant form of the house, by providing a strong horizontal feel, a light, airy feeling, a series of cascading forms, or a repetition of vertical forms.

Design Guidelines

A deck should have a special unifying element. A well-designed deck has a delightful and appealing quality, a special something that makes you want to walk onto it and stay awhile. This appeal comes from all elements working together to create a unified whole. But it also depends on some feature or theme that brings these elements together. It may be a continuous fascia board wrapped around the deck, the repetition of a railing motif, or the use of a continuous bench or planter. It should be a simple and basic element, one that reflects a similar feature in the house or nearby garden structures.

A related feature of good deck design is a strong focal point, an eye-catcher to which everything else is oriented. It could be an object on the deck, such as a piece of furniture, a sculpture, or a large plant. Or it could be a panoramic view from one side of the deck. The more simple the deck design, the greater chance of a clear focal point without conflicting points of interest.

A final issue related to the sense of unity in a deck and garden design is to avoid complex or overly ambitious designs. Concentrate on quality rather than quantity, doing only a few things, but doing them well.

Below: *The repetition of a decking pattern and a continuous line of benches pull this large, rambling deck together into one continuous whole.*

Right: *A broad vista provides the dominant focal point for this deck. Although it spreads onto several levels, the deck maintains a unified and harmonious feeling because of the continuity of color, railings, and benches. Angled decking boards reinforce the line of vision toward the most appealing view, and colored cushions and flowers provide interesting design accents.*

TWELVE DECK PLANS

This chapter features plans for 12 decks. Each plan is complete and ready to build, and even includes a full materials list. The structural details conform to most model building codes, but you should check them with your local building department and get proper permits before starting any construction.

The plans progress from low ground-huggers to more complex structures. Each deck is designed for a specific site, but it can be adapted to any number of locations to suit varying conditions. The plans are intended to reflect design principles that make each deck more than just an outdoor activity space.

Together, these deck plans also offer an encyclopedia of construction details. Even if you do not plan to build a particular deck, you may find the details useful for adapting another plan or even designing your own deck. The plans will help you see how footings, structural components, decking surfaces, railings, stairs, benches, and trim details interconnect with one another in a complete deck.

Although each plan is complete and is intended to be used by itself, you may find it helpful to go through all the plans. The techniques and details that are presented for the simpler designs will make the more complex designs easier to understand. You may also find ways to combine components from various decks.

A successful deck does not have to be an intricate and complex structure. The simple shapes of the deck shown here help it blend into its setting. Its stepped platforms define activity areas more clearly and provide a graceful transition to the garden. Each part of the deck is also appropriately scaled for its intended activities, giving a sense of pleasing proportion.

PLAN 1
Modular Sections for Quick Decks

Here is a simple deck system that features modular deck sections that can be laid directly on the ground or on a level surface such as a patio, pool area, or even a rooftop. It functions more like a patio than a raised deck, and its low profile helps retain privacy and create a sense of intimacy with the surrounding garden. You can change its shape and size to meet various needs by recombining sections into different shapes.

This kind of deck system has a wide range of applications. It can be the main deck in a small yard or the secondary deck in a large yard, where it can serve as a landscaping accent or as a simple way of using a forgotten corner. It might be the perfect way to transform an unused roof-

top into a pleasant garden retreat. It could also be used for a temporary or seasonal deck because the modules are portable and can be stacked for easy storage during winter.

Because it has no structural system of its own, it requires a level area that is stable and uniformly flat. It may also move and shift over time, although this problem is easily solved by making periodic adjustments, by toenailing the sections together, or by installing the deck over long sleepers. However, soils that are highly expansive may not be appropriate for this type of deck.

The following four pages provide ideas and techniques for installing a modular deck, whether you build your own or use prefabricated sections. There are instructions for in-

stalling deck modules on the ground, on concrete or masonry patios, and on rooftops. Each application features one of two types of modules, but you can use either of the designs for any installation.

Materials List

For 12 modular sections, set on sleepers

Base	108 sq ft 4-mil polyethylene sheeting (for weed control)		
	1 cu yd sand or well-graded gravel		
Sleepers	2x4s	2	12' lengths
	2x6s	2	12' lengths
12 Modules	2x4s	33	12' lengths
	(cut into 35½" pieces)		
Nails	10# 10d HDG common		

The 3 by 3 Deck Modules

The deck shown on these pages is only one of an endless number of possible configurations. They are all based on a single 3-foot-square module that you can build yourself. The modules are easy to carry and do not have to be constructed at the deck site. You can even build them in your garage or basement.

You can build the modules in almost any size or shape (see page 23 for one option). If you want to build larger modules, just add more cleats. If you build smaller modules, there will be considerably more nailing and cutting, and more joints between sections.

Besides varying the size of the module, you can vary the size of lumber. If you need to reduce the overall weight or thickness of the deck, you can use 1 by 4 lumber for the decking. If you do, add a third cleat halfway between the other two. You may prefer 2 by 3 or even 2 by 2 decking for a finely textured pattern. These sizes also require three cleats.

Building the Modules

Materials

Use pressure-treated lumber for the cleats, which make contact with the ground or other surfaces. For the 2 by 4 decking boards, use either pressure-treated lumber or naturally durable wood. Since they span almost 30 inches, the boards should be a structural grade of lumber that has few and relatively small knots, for maximum strength.

Cutting

Because all pieces are the same length, you may find it easiest to have your supplier cut them for you. Otherwise, note that the 35½-inch length requires two cuts for each 6-foot board, rather than simply cutting them in half. When cutting pressure-treated lumber, wear safety goggles, gloves, and a breathing mask.

Assembly

To construct each module, build a *nailing jig* as shown. Place nine of the 2 by 4s inside the jig, with their best-looking faces down. Lay the two cleats over them as shown, and nail.

Before nailing, be sure each 2 by 4 decking board is aligned for proper spacing. To avoid splitting the decking boards, especially with the nails so close to their ends, drill nail holes or blunt the point of each nail before nailing.

After assembling the modules, nail ½-inch plywood scraps on two sides of the module, as shown, to provide uniform spacing between modules. Some modules will not need spacers, so you may wait to attach the scraps until you decide on a final configuration. See pages 88-89 for details about finishing decks.

Constructing 3 by 3 Modules

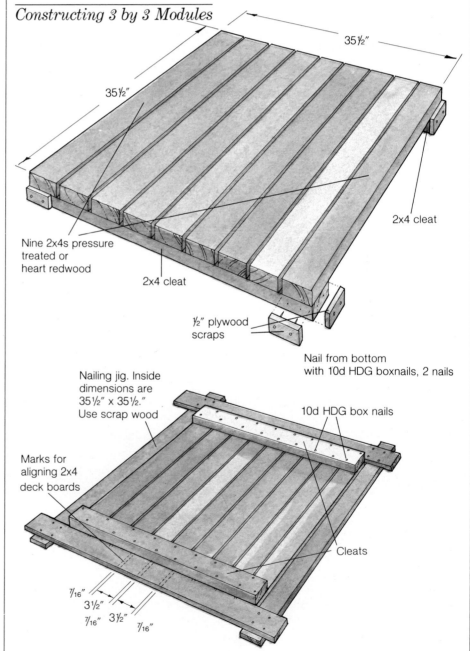

35½"

35½"

2x4 cleat

Nine 2x4s pressure treated or heart redwood

2x4 cleat

½" plywood scraps

Nail from bottom with 10d HDG boxnails, 2 nails

Nailing jig. Inside dimensions are 35½" x 35½." Use scrap wood

10d HDG box nails

Marks for aligning 2x4 deck boards

Cleats

7/16" 3½" 7/16" 3½" 7/16"

Installing the Deck Modules on the Ground

A wood deck that is placed directly on the ground will not last indefinitely, even under the most ideal conditions. But if you follow the methods outlined here, you should get years of service from your deck. Before you build, be sure that a deck placed directly on the ground is not prohibited by local codes. Usually, this type of deck is allowed as long as it is not attached to the house and is constructed of approved materials.

Materials

When constructing the deck modules, use only pressure-treated or naturally durable lumber suitable for ground contact. Do not rely on applying preservatives yourself, since the limited penetration offers only temporary protection for use at or below grade. However, it is a good practice to brush or soak the ends of cut boards with an approved preservative when you use pressure-treated lumber, to ensure even longer life.

Site Preparation

The most important feature of this deck's construction is the surface it rests on. Choose a site with good drainage. To prevent damp wood and shifting boards, excavate a shallow depression and fill it with a 3-inch layer of gravel or crushed rock. As a control for weeds, apply either a chemical growth retardant or a layer of 4-mil polyethylene sheeting before putting down the gravel. Puncture the sheeting every 2 or 3 feet to provide drain holes. (See page 25 for a method of adding a concrete or brick border around the excavation.)

Installation

Lay out string lines to guide placement of the sleepers and modules. Because work proceeds from the center outward, lay out center axes rather than perimeter string lines (see illustration). Level the gravel by screeding it with one of the 2 by 6

sleepers. Then lay the sleepers in place, following the spacings shown in the illustration. Set the modules in place, starting in the center and working outward, using the plywood shims for even spacing. For extra rigidity, toenail the modules to the sleepers. To unify the deck with a border and to cover the sleepers and cleats, nail 1 by 4 or 2 by 4 fascia boards around the perimeter. Use miter joints at the corners for a more finished look.

Installation for a Patio or Pool Deck

To cover an existing patio or pool area, place the wooden modules directly on the paving. For a permanent installation, and to prevent slipping, attach the perimeter sections with exterior construction adhesive.

Because the concrete subsurface is very rigid, you can construct the modules with 1-by lumber. This gives the deck a slim profile. Be sure to use a high-stress grade of lumber to ensure structural integrity.

Sleeper System for Installing Modules on the Ground

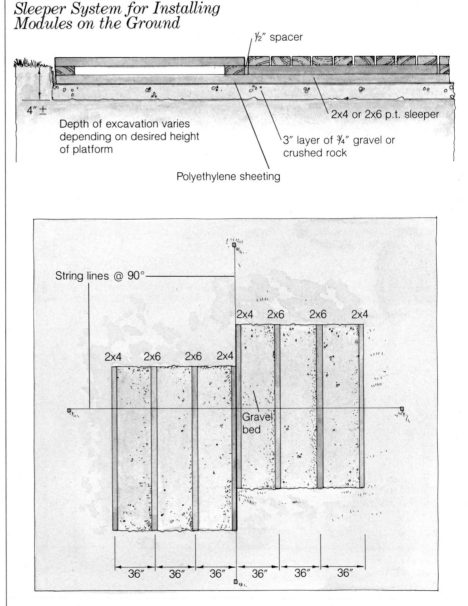

½" spacer

4" ±

Depth of excavation varies depending on desired height of platform

2x4 or 2x6 p.t. sleeper

3" layer of ¾" gravel or crushed rock

Polyethylene sheeting

String lines @ 90°

2x4   2x6   2x6   2x4

2x4   2x6   2x6   2x4

Gravel bed

36"   36"   36"   36"   36"   36"

Installing Deck Modules on a Roof

Rooftops offer an exciting option for outdoor living, and a modular deck system is the ideal candidate for such applications. Modules can be built at a more convenient location and transported to the rooftop, they can be moved for roof maintenance, and they can easily be expanded.

Preparation

Before considering a rooftop deck, however, here are some conditions that must be satisfied. First, will the roof support the weight of the deck? Most residential roofs are designed to support only their own weight. A roof intended as living space must be able to support an additional 30 or 40 pounds per square foot live load. Roofs on large buildings may already have a framing system that can handle the extra load, but you should hire a professional consultant to determine this for you or to recommend structural changes.

The roof should be in sound condition and should have a slope of at least ¼ inch per foot so that puddles won't form. Flashings should be sound, especially at parapets or other walls. Another consideration is access. It may be more bother to construct a stairway or roof hatch than to build a deck elsewhere. Or it could be a simple matter of changing a window into a door. Because walking on nondeck areas can damage roof membranes, be sure the access leads directly to your deck. You also need to consider safety requirements, such as railings or parapets and protection from nearby power lines. Finally, if you intend to do any gardening, you'll need a water faucet handy.

If these conditions can be met, you are ready to construct deck modules and install them on your roof. This is an ideal project to approach as a cooperative venture, pooling resources and efforts with your neighbors to develop a pleasant outdoor space that you can enjoy together.

Construction

The modules featured in this plan are different from those on the previous page, but you could use either design. These larger modules distribute the loads better and are less likely to shift around. They use 2 by 6s instead of 2 by 4s, but they are constructed the same way. The only difference is that the cleats are set in from the edge of the module rather than flush with it (see page 21).

You can use 1 by 6 decking boards to reduce overall weight or 2 by 4s for a finer texture, but they will require a third cleat.

Installation

The modules can be set directly on most roof surfaces, although gravel should be swept away and strips of 45-pound felt placed under the cleats. The modules will slope the same as the roof. If you want to level them, use long sleepers and place shims under the sleepers.

Choose an area of the roof that drains well. It should also have a protective parapet, railing, or other safety barrier and be close to an access door. Simply lay each section in place, and presto! . . . instant deck. Planters should be placed off the deck to maximize usable space.

A 3' by 6' Deck Module

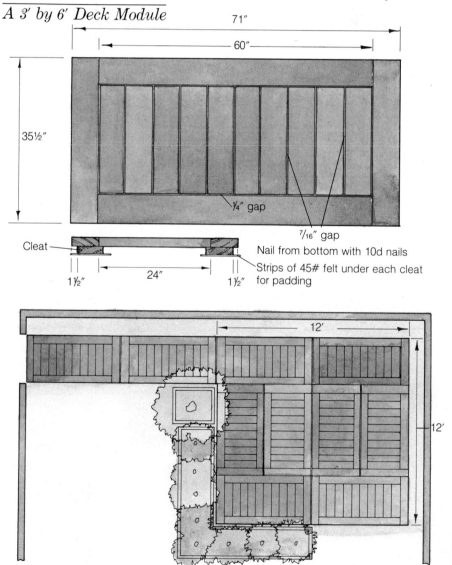

71"

60"

35½"

¼" gap

⁷⁄₁₆" gap

Nail from bottom with 10d nails

Cleat

Strips of 45# felt under each cleat for padding

1½" 24" 1½"

12'

12'

PLAN 2
An Elegant Deck Flush with the Ground

This plan features another ground-level deck that is easy to build and can be adapted to a variety of settings, including installations directly on the ground, over an existing patio, or on a rooftop. Unlike the modular decks in Plan 1, it is a unified structure that is less likely to shift or settle. It also uses full-length decking boards, giving it a more restful appearance.

The L-shaped deck featured on these pages is ideal for a transition area, between the house and lawn for instance. It provides a usable space away from the main traffic corridor, where a table or a pair of lounge chairs invite casual relaxing. Plantings along the side borders help to confine the space.

By lowering the deck into a shallow excavation and edging it with a masonry or concrete border, you can give it a touch of refined elegance. A wood surface that is level with the ground creates a dignified and dramatic landscape element.

Plan View

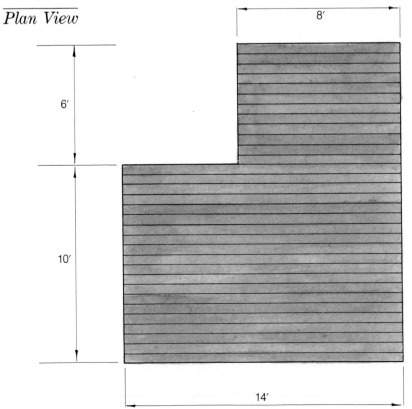

Construction Techniques

This deck can be built directly on or below grade, as long as you prepare the site carefully and use pressure-treated lumber or other lumber suitable for ground contact. You can alter the size and shape of this deck very easily by changing the lengths of the decking boards and the lengths and spacings of the sleepers.

Site Preparation

Choose a site that drains well naturally, or be prepared to install subsurface drain pipes. Lay out the perimeter of the deck and excavate. The illustrations below show that the depth of the excavation varies with the height of the deck. Deeper excavations should have a solid border of concrete or brick to retain the edges, and you should install it before you install the deck. After excavating, provide for weed control (see page 22), and install the gravel.

Sleepers and Decking

Cut 4 by 4s to length for the sleepers and lay them on the gravel bed. You can use 2 by 4s or 2 by 6s to reduce the thickness of the deck, but they provide less clearance for air circulation and give less structural rigidity. The sleeper spacing on this deck is 42 inches, which requires the strength of 2 by 5 decking boards. If you use 2 by 4s or smaller deck boards, add more sleepers. Space sleepers for 2 by 4 decking no more than 24 inches apart; for 1-inch decking, space them no more than 16 inches apart.

Nail the decking boards with two 12ds or 16d corrosion-resistant nails at each sleeper (use three nails for 6-inch boards), using a string line or straightedge to ensure a straight, even line of exposed nail heads. You can lay the boards diagonally or in a herringbone pattern (see page 78), but if you do, the actual spans for the decking boards will be greater than the sleeper spacings. To compensate, place the sleepers closer together.

Trim and Finish

Place any border around the excavation before building the deck. Nail 2 by 4 fascia boards around the perimeter of above-grade decks. Stain or paint the deck after it has seasoned.

Materials List

Base	200 sq ft 4-mil polyethylene sheeting		
	1.75 cu yd ¾" gravel		
Sleepers	4x4s	2	10' lengths
		3	16' lengths
Decking	2x6s	12	8' lengths
		20	14' lengths (188 sq ft)
Nails	7#		12d HDG common
Curb Options	A) Fascia		
	2x4s	2	6' lengths
		1	10' length
		1	14' length
		1	16' length
		1	18' length
	B) Concrete		
	1 cu yd concrete		
	120' 1x8 (for forms) (8"x8"x60')		
	C) Brick		
	½ cu yd concrete		
	360 common bricks and mortar		

Laying Out Sleepers

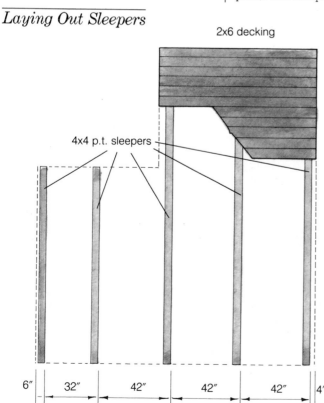

2x6 decking

4x4 p.t. sleepers

6" 32" 42" 42" 42" 4"

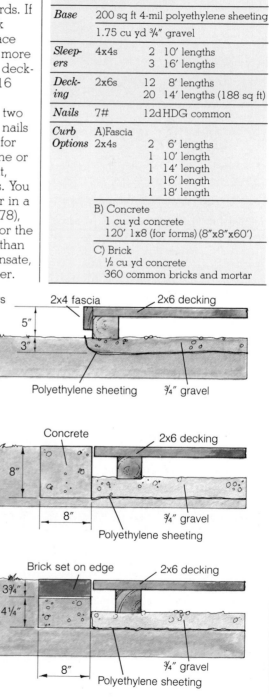

Options for borders

2x4 fascia 2x6 decking
5"
3"
Polyethylene sheeting ¾" gravel

Concrete 2x6 decking
8"
8" ¾" gravel
Polyethylene sheeting

Brick set on edge 2x6 decking
3¾"
4¼"
8" ¾" gravel
Polyethylene sheeting

PLAN 3
A New Deck for an Old Patio

A sleeper deck system is a great way to cover an existing patio. Although patios are certainly a useful and pleasing design element for any landscape, some patios may be too small, may absorb too much heat from the sun, or may be cracked and damaged. Covering a patio with a deck might be easier than replacing it, and you may prefer the color, texture, and line patterns of natural wood over the appearance of concrete or masonry.

The deck featured in this plan is for a condominium with a small yard and a correspondingly small patio. The deck solves these problems by extending usable activity space beyond the patio. It provides a strong focal point for the yard and creates an inviting access to a shade garden or lawn, and to the gate. It has ample room for two separate activity areas, perhaps one for outdoor dining and the other for a conversation or reading area.

Construction Techniques

Site Preparation and Footings
A concrete or masonry patio is an excellent base for a deck, and it requires no special preparation. It should slope away from the house.

If you want to extend your deck beyond the patio, as this plan shows, you must provide bearing for the sleepers. If the patio is level and the area around it well drained, you may be able to prepare a gravel bed beyond the patio and lay sleepers directly on it (see page 25). More likely, the patio is sloped and the ground beyond it cannot easily be raised to its level. In this case, you'll need to provide concrete piers and footings for the sleepers. This plan shows typical dimensions for footings, although depths and sizes will vary according to local conditions. (Ortho's book *How to Design & Build Decks & Patios* describes techniques for building concrete footings.)

Because the sleepers will lie directly on the piers, with no posts, they all must be level with each other. The easiest way to ensure this is to form and build the piers and footings together rather than use precast piers.

Installing Sleepers
When laying sleepers on a patio, you can minimize warping by attaching them to the concrete with exterior construction adhesive, concrete nails, or expansion bolts designed for concrete. If the patio slopes, level each sleeper with shims. Nail the shims to the bottom of the sleeper first, and then turn it over and nail or glue the sleeper to the patio.

This plan uses 4 by 4 sleepers because they also act as beams. The spacing between footings (and therefore the number of footings) can be adjusted by using sleepers having a greater depth. Using sleeper material of a different size can also vary the height of the deck. In all cases, the lumber must be pressure-treated or naturally durable material, and long boards set directly on the patio should run parallel with the slope to avoid becoming dams that trap water.

The spacing between sleepers depends on the span limits of the decking. This plan uses 2 by 6s, which allow a wider distance between sleepers than 2 by 4s or 1-by lumber.

Installing Decking

Nail or glue the decking to the sleepers, as described on page 25. It is best to lay out all the boards first so you can adjust for any variations in appearance.

Trim and Finish

Nail 2 by 8 fascia boards around the exposed edges of the deck. Designs that use sleepers and decking thicker than those in this plan will require fascia material sized accordingly.

Materials List

Foot-ings	(Materials for 8; number can vary)		
	10.5 cu ft concrete {for 8 piers (8"x8"x8") and footings (12"x12"x12")}		
	8 metal post anchors		
	16 ⅜"x4½" carriage bolts with nuts and washers		
Sleep-ers	4x4s	2	8' lengths
		4	16' lengths
	Shims and scrap blocks		
	1 tube exterior construction adhesive		
Deck-ing	2x6s	16	14' lengths
		8	18' lengths (184 sq ft)
Fascia	2x8s	2	8' lengths
		1	14' length
Nails	8#	12d	HDG common

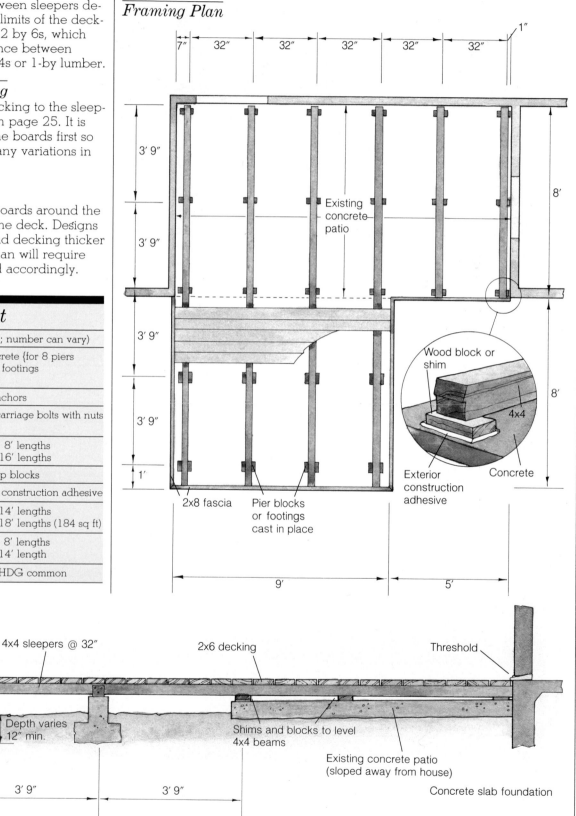

Framing Plan

7"   32"   32"   32"   32"   32"   1"

3' 9"

3' 9"

Existing concrete patio

8'

3' 9"

3' 9"

1'

2x8 fascia

Pier blocks or footings cast in place

Wood block or shim

4x4

Exterior construction adhesive

Concrete

8'

9'   5'

Section

2x8 fascia

4x4 sleepers @ 32"

2x6 decking

Threshold

Depth varies 12" min.

Shims and blocks to level 4x4 beams

Existing concrete patio (sloped away from house)

Concrete slab foundation

3' 9"   3' 9"

PLAN 4
A Simple Garden Platform

Plan View

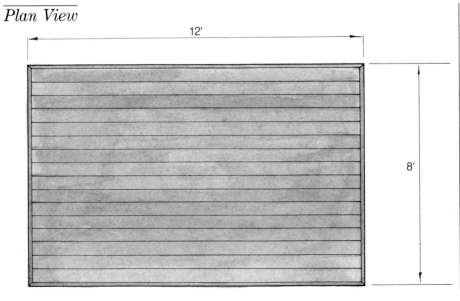

12'

8'

This freestanding deck is a permanent, raised platform that can go anywhere in a level yard. It is an ideal solution for a problem area, such as a drab corner that never seems to get used or an area unsuited for plants. Use it as a retreat, as a dining area, as a fantasy platform for children's play, as a planter display area, or for any other purpose requiring a level surface. Because it is wood, it blends well with your garden and will not overheat in direct sun. It is raised high enough to provide some detachment from other areas of the yard but low enough to maintain an intimate relationship with the surroundings and to retain the privacy provided by existing fences or shrubbery.

Because it is a simple rectangle, the deck can reflect other landscaping or architectural forms, such as fences, lawns, planting beds, and the house itself. However, locate it carefully so that its straight edges are oriented along an existing visual axis or axes. Otherwise, its size and strong form can make it look out of place or create a disturbing tension. Even when it is carefully aligned with existing visual axes, there is some danger of too many hard edges and straight lines if the landscape already has an abundance of geometric forms. The easiest solution to this problem is to soften the deck's edges with plantings around its perimeter. Another solution is to add a meandering pathway of curved pavers leading to the deck, or to alter the corners of the lawn or planting beds so they are curved rather than square.

The overall effect and visual impact of this deck are limited only by imagination. It can look stark and striking surrounded by an expanse of level lawn, or subtle and rich nestled into a grotto of trees in a remote corner of the yard.

Construction Techniques

This small platform is intended to be as low to the ground as possible and still maintain required clearances between earth and wood. Because it is not attached to the house, you may be able to reduce the clearance normally required for an attached structure. Check your local codes.

You achieve the low profile by hanging the joists between rather than on top of the beams, and by using 2 by 6 joists and beams. This limits the width of the deck to approximately 8 feet, but you can widen it by adding a third beam and a new set of 2 by 6 joists.

Framing Plan

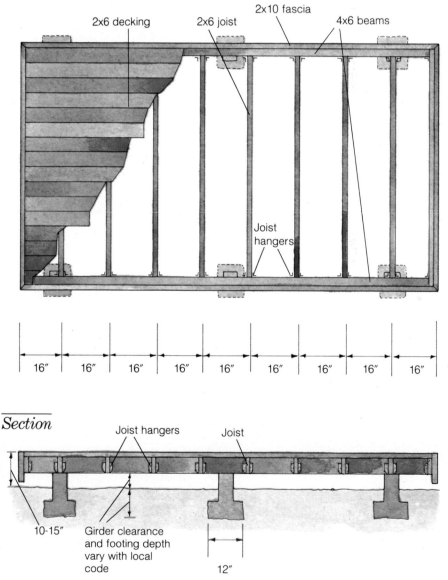

2x6 decking   2x6 joist   2x10 fascia   4x6 beams

Joist hangers

16″ 16″ 16″ 16″ 16″ 16″ 16″ 16″ 16″

Section

Joist hangers   Joist

10-15″   Girder clearance and footing depth vary with local code

12″

Materials List

Footings	15.5 cu ft concrete (for 6 piers (8″x8″x8″) and footings (18″x18″x12″)}		
	2x6s	6	blocks for piers
Framing	Beams 4x6s	2	12′ lengths
	Joists 2x6s	10	8′ lengths
	Joist hangers 2x6s	20	
Decking	2x6s	16	12′ lengths (96 sq ft)
Fascia	2x10s	2	8′ lengths
		2	12′ lengths
Nails		2#	joist hanger nails
		7#	12d HDG common
		5#	16d HDG common

PLAN 4

Layout and Footings

The piers for this deck are on the perimeter. Locate string lines so the outside edges of the piers will be flush with the outside face of the beams and so the fascia board can cover them. All piers must be level because the girders rest directly on them. To connect the piers and beams, use blocks of pressure-treated wood rather than metal post anchors, because wood blocks can be set flush with the outside edge of the pier and beam. Embed the blocks in the piers while the concrete is wet.

Beams and Joists

For a deck this close to the ground, all structural members should be pressure-treated lumber suitable for ground contact or all-heart grades of naturally durable lumber. Use high-quality corrosion-resistant nails, including the joist hanger nails, and leave a ¼-inch gap between the ends of the joists and the beams. The end joists are 7 inches longer than the others and are attached to the beam ends with face nailing rather than joist hangers. It may be necessary to excavate under some of the joists to provide adequate clearance.

Decking

This plan shows 2 by 6 decking, but because the joists are spaced 16 inches apart, you can use decking of smaller dimensions.

Fascia and Finish

The 2 by 10 fascia provides a skirt for the deck that hides the piers, keeps out leaves and debris, helps the deck hug the ground, and creates a finished border for the decking boards. If the deck is set into a shallow excavation and is therefore closer to the ground, you can use other sizes or thicknesses of lumber for the fascia, such as 1 by 12 or 2 by 8.

If the deck is more than 10 inches above grade, you should provide a low step. See page 86 for techniques.

Finish the deck as desired with stain, paint, or natural weathering.

A Simple Variation

This plan is a variation of the low platform shown on the previous two pages, with the boards running the short distance rather than long. Its shorter deck boards "widen" the short dimension and make the deck feel less like a corridor; this is an important feature where serenity and repose is important, as well as with elongated decks.

Construction Techniques

The structural system for this deck consists of only three beams. The beams are 4 by 8 instead of 4 by 6, so you need only two footings for each one. You can change the size of the deck by lengthening the beams or by adding new beams to widen it. With this system it is possible to make large platforms set low to the ground, although they require more footings than a joist-over-beam system.

Framing Plan

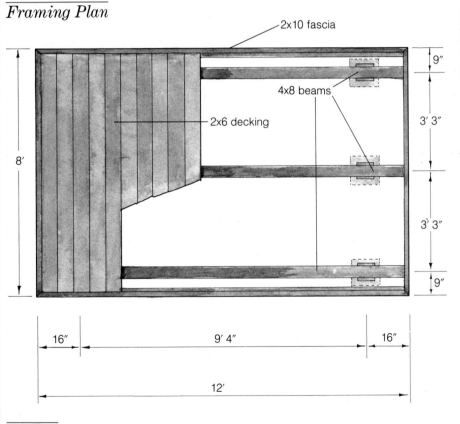

2x10 fascia
4x8 beams
2x6 decking
9"
3' 3"
3' 3"
9"
8'
16"
9' 4"
16"
12'

Section

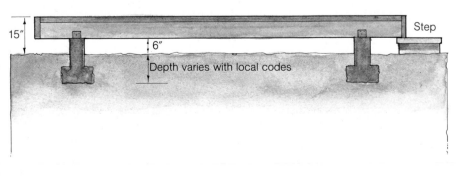

15"
6"
Depth varies with local codes
Step

Layout and Footings
Because the footings are set in from the perimeter, you can center the piers under the beams instead of setting them flush with the edges. All piers should be level with one another, because the beams rest directly on them.

Beams and Decking
Use pressure-treated or other decay-resistant lumber for the beams. Run the decking over their tops and nail. Use full 8-foot pieces and then trim them to 7 feet 9 inches, preferably along both sides to produce neat, straight edges. The 7-foot 9-inch length allows an 8-foot fascia board, but if you use longer fascia material, you needn't trim the decking.

Fascia and Finish
On this deck the fascia is more than decorative. It also stabilizes the overhanging ends of the deck boards, which might warp and twist. The fascia boards along the sides need to be connected to the decking as well as to each end of the short fascia boards. If you nail the fascia onto the ends of the decking boards, the large number of nails required will look like upholstery tacks. A solution for this problem is to nail a 2 by 4 cleat inside the fascia board before installing it and then nail the decking boards down onto the cleat. To temporarily stiffen the fascia against the downward pressure of this nailing, place a car jack or blocking under the section being nailed.

Because this deck uses deeper beams, it is 15 inches high and requires a low step. Running such a step along one entire side makes a nice bench for sitting, relaxing, or displaying plants. For construction details, see page 86.

An L-Shaped Combination
This plan shows one way to combine the two structural systems featured for low platforms. The result is an L-shaped deck that is large enough for both a transition walkway and a separate activity area. Note how the direction of the decking boards reinforces each function. Plantings help define the direction of flow, create a sense of closure, and define the grassy open space embraced by the deck.

This deck is really two decks similar to those on the preceding three pages. One section is supported by two 18-foot beams placed 6 feet apart, with 2 by 6 joists hung between them on 24-inch centers. The footings are 5 feet 6 inches on center.

The other section is identical to the deck on page 30, except that the girders are 4 by 6 instead of 4 by 8 and each one has three supports. Beam hangers attach the 12-foot beams to the 18-foot beam. Note that the center footings for the 12-foot beams are closer to the intersection (4 feet 6 inches) than to the end of the 8-foot-wide arm (7 feet 6 inches).

A long, low step along the edge of the grass completes this deck, providing easy access to the grass as well as additional sitting or display space. Use 2 by 6 fascia on the deck's edge so the step can tuck under it, making the deck appear to float out over the step.

Plan View

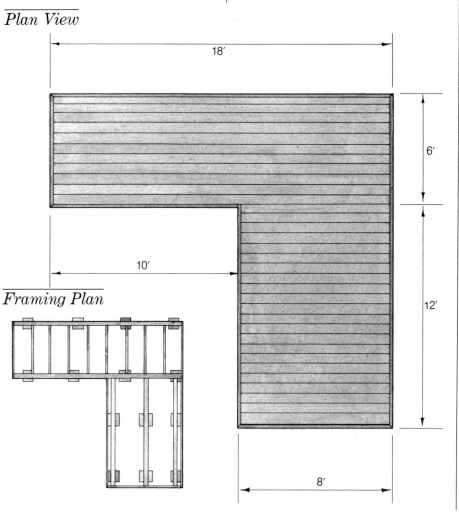

Framing Plan

PLAN 5
A Floating Deck for Gentle Slopes

This deck is the perfect solution for a neglected sloping corner of the yard or for small yards that have no level space. It could even be lengthened to extend across an entire backyard that slopes away from the house. It is featured on a gentle slope here, but the same structure could easily be adapted for steeper slopes by lengthening the posts and increasing the footing depths. A railing would be required along any side of the deck that is more than 30 inches above the ground, or whatever your local code requires. For gentle slopes, a bench is sufficient protection, if needed.

Access to the deck is easiest from the uphill side, so it is most appropriate for yards that slope away from the house or main part of the garden. To make the approach cleaner and the deck even more accessible, you could build a simple retaining wall of masonry or pressure-treated timbers along the uphill edge of the deck.

One or more steps would be required for approaches from the downhill side.

The joist-and-beam structure of this deck allows the footings to be set back from all the edges 1 to 2 feet, or even more with larger-sized lumber. This conceals the piers and posts, making the deck appear to float.

This effect creates interesting possibilities for breaking up flat space, accenting horizontal planes, or extending level areas. Although this plan features the deck on sloping ground, it can be built on level ground as well. The next page shows a possible setting for this deck in a level yard.

Plan
View

18'

18"

12'

A Floating Deck for Level Ground

Here is the same deck used as a freestanding platform in a level yard. Its structural system makes it higher than the lower deck in Plan 3; but for a very large deck, it has the advantage of fewer footings. Its overhangs also create a hovering effect that gives you an interesting perspective of the surrounding garden. Since it is not high enough to require a railing, it provides both contact and detachment at the same time. It should be built on a generous enough site so that you feel safe.

Access is provided by a step and transition platform. Other possibilities might be a bridge from the house or from part of the yard, or you might want to attach the deck to the house. See page 44 for specific techniques.

Construction Techniques

The structural system of joists resting on beams is a common and versatile approach to deck framing and is used for most of the designs in this book. You can move the footings in from the edges of the deck, redesign the structure for varying conditions without changing the size of the deck, or adapt it to any change in the deck's overall size or shape. For instance, this deck has three beams in order to use 2 by 6 joists for their low profile. However, if you wish to reduce the number of footings or to increase the deck's thickness, you could use 2 by 8 joists, 16 inches on center, and only two beams.

Layout and Footings

To mark the footing locations, stretch three string lines to represent the edges of the beams, and another to represent one end of the deck. You will need these lines later to install posts. Use layout techniques for slopes, which means measuring all distances along a level plane rather than along sloping ground.

When excavating for footings on a slope, dig the holes slightly deeper than the code requirements for level ground (2 or 3 inches for gentle slopes). Always measure the depth of the hole from the downhill edge.

In spite of being on a slope, the footings and piers for this deck are easier to build than the ones for the previous plan because only those for the top beam have to be level with each other. Later, you can cut each post to length. Just make sure the pier blocks or metal anchors for each beam are in perfect alignment.

Posts, Beams, and Joists

Install the top beam first, attaching it directly to its three piers. Use shims to level it. Then install posts for the other two beams. Cut the posts slightly long before installing them, rather than cutting them to exact length. If the posts are not made of pressure-treated lumber, you should soak their bottoms in an approved preservative. When the posts are in place, plumb them and nail temporary diagonal braces to them. Then level each post to the bottom of the top beam and mark the post for cutting.

Align the ends of all the beams with the string line, and attach girders to the posts with metal connectors. Then toenail the 2 by 6 joists to the beams. Install blocking over the center beam and rim joists along both sides. Trim the joist ends for a straight, clean edge. Install the rim joists the same day as the field joist. Otherwise, their ends may warp.

Decking and Fascia

Nail or glue the decking boards. When you get to the 2 by 8 bench uprights, provide support for the decking boards by nailing a wood cleat onto the side of each upright opposite the joist it is bolted to. Then either notch a long deck board or cut short lengths of decking to fit between the uprights. Finish out the deck with a full-length board.

The fascia's top edge is flush with the decking surface. This plan uses 2 by 8s to maintain a sleek look, but if you want to conceal more of the understructure, or if you are using deeper joists than 2 by 6s, you can use wider fascia boards. You can use a 2 by 12 fascia to hide the beam ends, or you can bevel them.

Bench

Any bench design can be used for this deck, but the one shown is very sturdy and gives a simple, clean look to the deck. When you install the 2 by 8 uprights, be sure they are all level. The easiest way is to mark each one exactly 18 inches from the top and align this mark along the top edge of the joist when bolting it. Then cut the 2 by 4 cleats, beveling each end so it doesn't protrude below the 2 by 4 trim piece. Bolt them in place so they are centered on the 2 by 8 upright and level.

Nail 2 by 2s into the cleats, blind nailing from the sides so the nails don't show. Predrill before nailing into any ends. When all the 2 by 2s are in place, trim their ends. Then install the 2 by 4 trim boards by nailing them into the cleats. Miter the corners for a more finished look.

Materials List

Footings	23 cu ft concrete {for 9 piers (8"x8"x8") and footing (18"x18"x12")}			
	9 metal post anchors			
	18 ⅜"x4½" carriage bolts with nuts and washers			
Framing	Posts	4x4s	1	8' length (for 6 short posts; length will vary)
	Beams	4x6s	3	18' lengths
	Joists	2x6s	10	12' lengths
	Blocking	2x6s	1	18' length (cut into 9 22½" ± pieces)
Decking		2x6s	24	18' lengths (216 sq ft)
Fascia		2x8s	2	12' lengths
		2x8s	2	18' lengths
Bench	Uprights	2x8s	2	10' lengths (cut into 10 23½ pieces)
	Cleats	2x4s	1	14' length (cut into 10 15" pieces)
	Seat	2x2s	9	18' lengths
	Trim	2x4s	2	20' lengths
	Bolts	20		⁵⁄₁₆"x3½" carriage bolts with nuts and washers
		20		⅜"x3½" carriage bolts with nuts and washers
Nails		5#		8d HDG box or finish (for bench)
		10#		12d HDG common
		7#		16d HDG common

Footing and Framing Plan

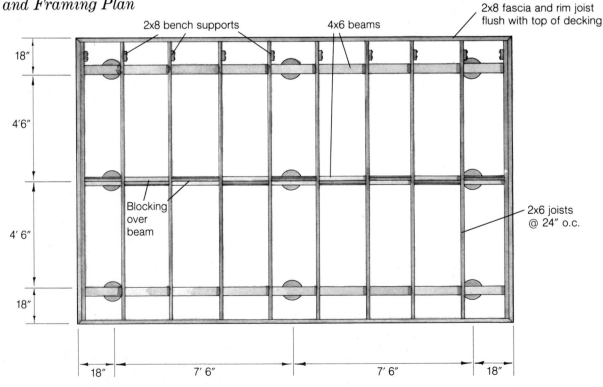

2x8 bench supports

4x6 beams

2x8 fascia and rim joist flush with top of decking

18"

4'6"

Blocking over beam

4' 6"

2x6 joists @ 24" o.c.

18"

18"   7' 6"   7' 6"   18"

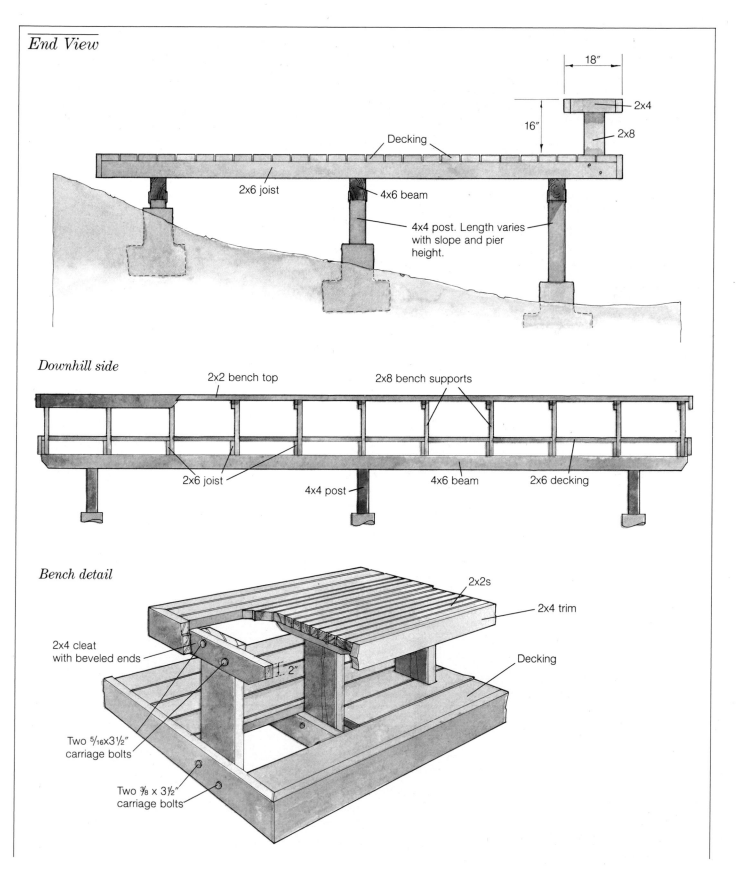

End View

18″

2x4

16″

2x8

Decking

2x6 joist

4x6 beam

4x4 post. Length varies with slope and pier height.

Downhill side

2x2 bench top

2x8 bench supports

2x6 joist

4x4 post

4x6 beam

2x6 decking

Bench detail

2x2s

2x4 trim

2x4 cleat with beveled ends

2″

Decking

Two 5/16x3½″ carriage bolts

Two 3/8 x 3½″ carriage bolts

PLAN 6
Multilevel Platforms for the Garden

If you plan to build a large deck, there are several reasons for dividing it into two or more platforms on different levels. For one thing, stepped platforms create variety and interest by breaking up a monotonous surface. They also define separate spaces for different uses, such as eating, relaxing, visiting, working, children's play, and so on. If the yard is sloped, the stepped structure keeps all parts of the deck close to the ground, creating a cascade effect and eliminating the need for railings. Stepped platforms are particularly effective for decks that are upslope from the house or main areas of the yard because they help make the deck feel accessible without being prohibitively tall. Finally, the variety of shapes actually make the deck feel larger than a single platform of equivalent square footage, as long as each part of the deck is ample enough for at least two chairs and a table.

The deck featured in this plan has two platforms separated by an intermediate step. You can eliminate the step and separate the platforms by only one change in level, or add an additional platform for even greater height separation; however, the single step works very well in this plan because it provides a wide enough platform to stretch out on or to walk along. This subtle invitation to explore the deck adds to its appeal.

There is an important safety consideration with any kind of steps or changes in level on decks: they are often hard to see because they blend in with the strong pattern of decking boards, especially one-step changes in level. This deck solves that problem by making a two-step change in levels and by trimming the steps with 2 by 4 fascia. You can also run the decking boards in different directions for each level and provide a handrail.

This deck works well situated against a fence, either in level yards or in yards that slope up away from the house. Because it is accessible from two sides, you have many options for giving it the closure or openness you desire. In this example, white gravel reinforces the sense of graciousness and serenity.

Structural Features

This deck's two main platforms have different structural systems in order to keep the lower platform as close to the ground as possible and to provide enough height difference for a transition step. The lower platform uses 4 by 6 beams with the minimum earth-wood clearance for the lowest possible platform using a reasonable number of footings. The upper platform uses a beam-and-joist structure that is approximately 28 to 30 inches above grade. This is generally the maximum height allowed for decks without railings.

Structurally, the platforms and steps are all connected to each other. Some multilevel decks have platforms that are independent of each other, but this design creates an integral structure to simplify the leveling process and to ensure uniform step dimensions. The steps in this deck are all 7½ inches high, a height created by using 2 by 8 and 4 by 8 framing members in the upper platform. You can reduce the height of each step to 5½ inches by using 2 by 6 and 4 by 6 framing members throughout the deck. If you do this, you will have to add a third beam to the upper deck to support the 2 by 6 joists.

Design variations for this deck are unlimited; simply extend or shorten the sides, change dimensions, or change the basic shape. Page 41 shows you an option for changing the pattern of the decking boards.

This pattern features a border around the outside of the lower deck. The change in direction of the boards for this border requires a modification of the framing underneath. A framing plan is included to show you the changes.

Other design variations include making the steps broader by extending their supporting joists, enlarging the deck platforms, and changing the footing design by altering the depth or shape of the piers.

If the upper platform needs a safety barrier, you could attach railing posts to the rim joists or build a bench.

Plan View

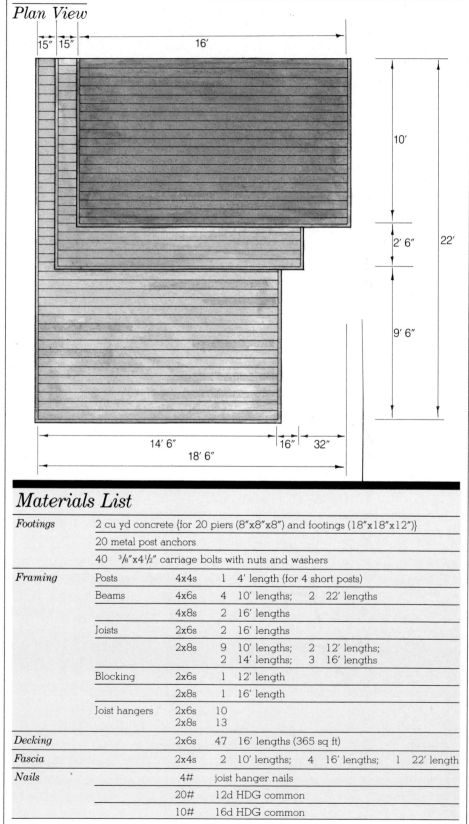

Materials List

Footings	2 cu yd concrete {for 20 piers (8"x8"x8") and footings (18"x18"x12")}			
	20 metal post anchors			
	40 ⅜"x4½" carriage bolts with nuts and washers			
Framing	Posts	4x4s	1	4' length (for 4 short posts)
	Beams	4x6s	4	10' lengths; 2 22' lengths
		4x8s	2	16' lengths
	Joists	2x6s	2	16' lengths
		2x8s	9	10' lengths; 2 12' lengths; 2 14' lengths; 3 16' lengths
	Blocking	2x6s	1	12' length
		2x8s	1	16' length
	Joist hangers	2x6s	10	
		2x8s	13	
Decking		2x6s	47	16' lengths (365 sq ft)
Fascia		2x4s	2	10' lengths; 4 16' lengths; 1 22' length
Nails			4#	joist hanger nails
			20#	12d HDG common
			10#	16d HDG common

Construction Techniques

Layout and Footings

This deck has 20 footings, and except for the 4 that have posts, they should all be level with each other. The footing and beam plan gives all the dimensions needed for laying out the footing locations.

The plans for this deck show the column style of piers—chosen for their ease of construction—that are formed with fiber tubes, but any style is fine. The depth of the footings will vary with local codes and conditions.

You may want to excavate shallow trenches where all the low beams will be located to ensure proper clearance. This way, you keep the deck low relative to the rest of the yard.

Beams and Joists

Use higher-stress structural grades of lumber because the spans are all close to maximum for the size lumber being used. Use pressure-treated or heart grades of naturally durable species of lumber for the 4 by 6 beams. Two of these beams extend the full 22-foot length of the deck.

Install the 4 by 6 beams first, because one end of each upper beam rests on one of the 4 by 6s. Use metal connectors for this attachment. You will also have to cut short posts or blocks to level the upper beams on their piers. Use metal connectors for attaching the beams to these posts.

The joists can be toenailed or attached to the beams with framing clips. When you attach the rim joists, nail the lower nails carefully, since they will be visible underneath the 2 by 4 fascia. Use an attractive grade of lumber for the rim joists, or plan to stain them a dark color to enhance the shadow line.

Stair Framing

The intermediate step and lower step are framed with short joists hung on joist hangers. When you measure them for cutting, subtract ¼ to ⅛ inch to provide a gap at each end for air circulation. Nail the joist hangers

to the joist first. Then set it in place and nail the hangers to the beam or stringer. This way you can be sure the top of the joist will be flush with the top of the beam. Complete the stair framing before installing the joists for the upper platform.

Decking and Fascia

The deck boards are 2 by 6s in order to span the 3-foot beam spacings. Nail the boards on the lower platform by starting at the end and working toward the step. You may have to rip the last board to fit. Start the step and

top platform from the edge closest to the lower platform. Do not overhang the first board; start it flush with the rim joist.

Predrill all the short pieces before you nail them to avoid splitting their ends. When all the decking is nailed in place, trim the ends flush with the edges of the beams or joists.

The 2 by 4 fascia boards make the platforms appear to float out over each other. Page 40 shows a detail for creating even more of an overhang to achieve this floating effect.

Footing and Beam Plan
(All dimensions are center to center)

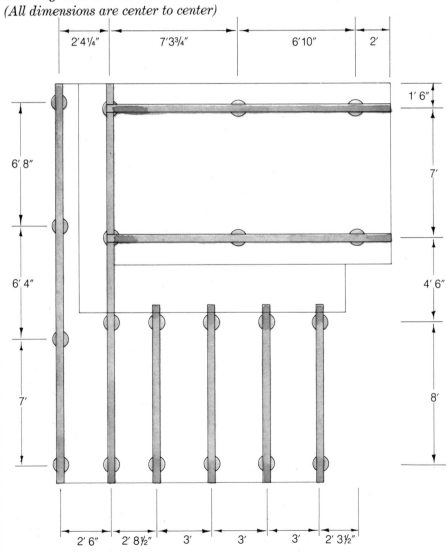

Footing and Framing Plan

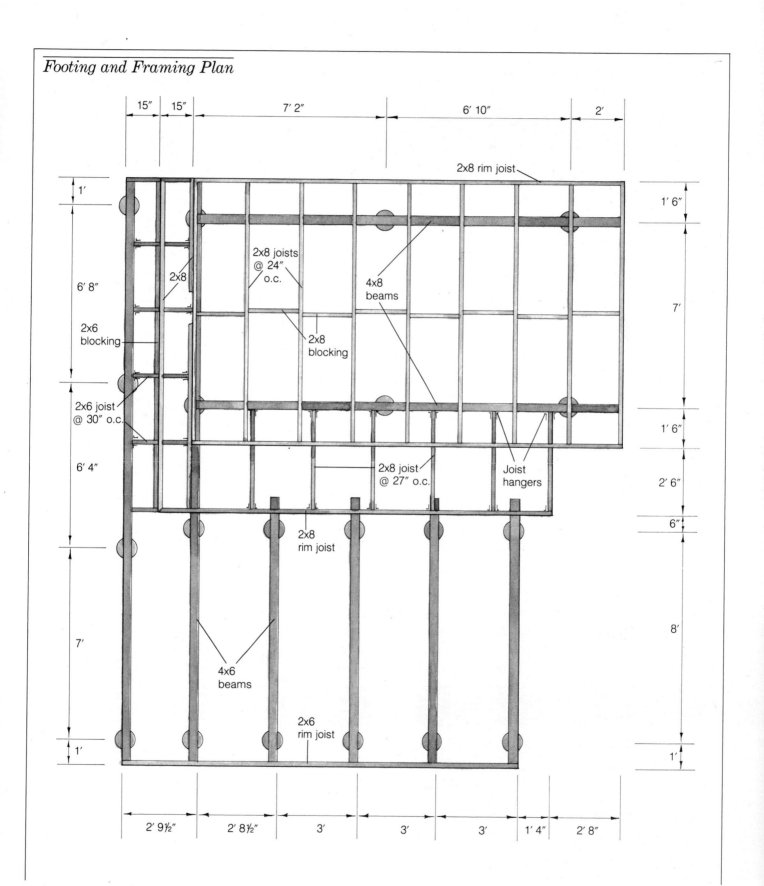

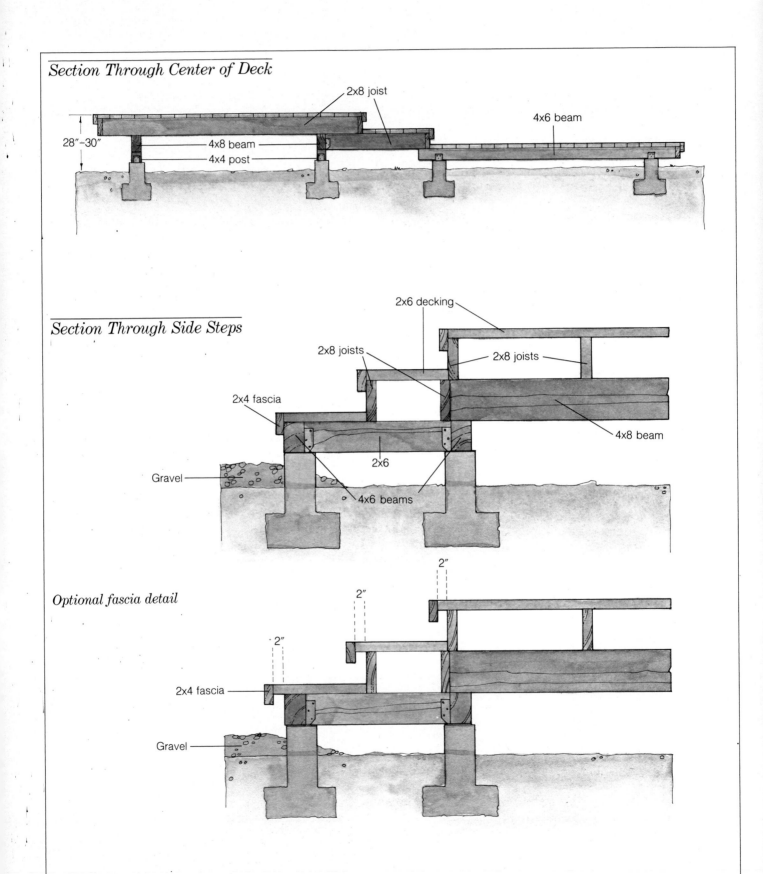

Section Through Center of Deck

2x8 joist

4x6 beam

28″–30″

4x8 beam

4x4 post

Section Through Side Steps

2x6 decking

2x8 joists

2x8 joists

2x4 fascia

4x8 beam

Gravel

2x6

4x6 beams

Optional fascia detail

2″

2″

2″

2x4 fascia

Gravel

A Variation of Decking Pattern

Use this plan for long decking boards instead of short ones. The boards of the bottom step extend to become a border around the lower platform.

The framing diagram shows the same footing locations, beam structure, and upper platform joists as the plan on page 39. The major changes are the addition of short joists between the outer beams of the lower platform and between the joists along the left side of the upper step. All blocking and diagonal joists support joints in the decking.

Plan 6 Variation

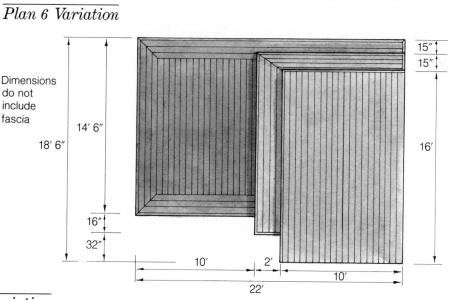

Dimensions do not include fascia

15"
15"
18' 6"
14' 6"
16"
32"
16'
10'
2'
10'
22'

Footing and Framing Plan for Variation

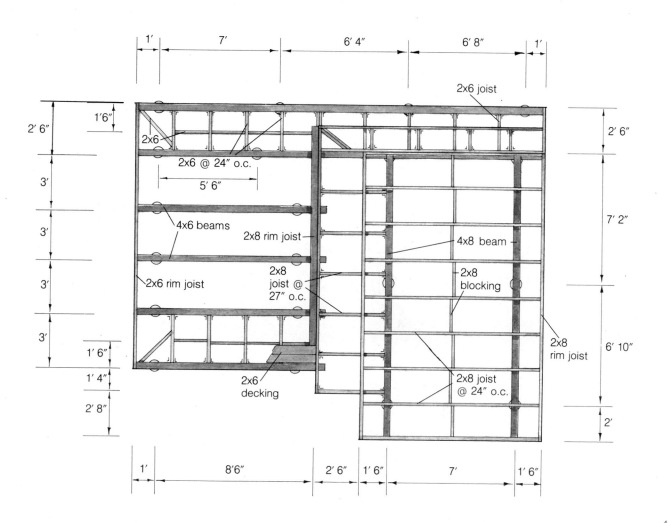

1'   7'   6' 4"   6' 8"   1'

2x6 joist
2' 6"
1'6"
2' 6"
2x6
2x6 @ 24" o.c.
5' 6"
3'
7' 2"
3'
4x6 beams
2x8 rim joist
4x8 beam
2x8 blocking
3'
2x6 rim joist
2x8 joist @ 27" o.c.
2x8 rim joist
3'
1'6"
6' 10"
1' 4"
2x6 decking
2x8 joist @ 24" o.c.
2' 8"
2'

1'   8'6"   2' 6"   1' 6"   7'   1' 6"

PLAN 7
An Engawa

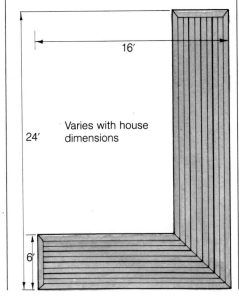

The *engawa* is a Japanese-inspired deck that is really a simple walkway around the house. Like other decks attached to the house, it is an outdoor extension of living space. However, it is not an activity area with a strictly utilitarian function; rather, its size and proportions suggest quiet and detached observation or gentle movement. The appeal of an engawa is its intimacy with adjacent plants and garden features, inviting one to bend over and touch them or to sit and relax close to them.

The engawa in this example is 6 feet wide, ample room for stretching and relaxing or for two people to walk side by side. The wide deck boards also contribute to a feeling of serenity and simplicity. It has access from both ends, which is important to allow leisurely flow. The sliding door opens onto the side rather than the end of the deck, a subtle feature that takes advantage of the direction of the decking boards. When you step onto the deck, your path is gently opposed by the decking pattern as well as the very short distance to the edge, immediately slowing your pace and rhythm.

This deck is the perfect complement for a small enclosed garden. Because it is at floor level, it is very convenient and inviting, giving the feeling that you can be in your garden without even leaving your room. Staining or painting it to match the house contributes to the feeling of unity and harmony.

Plan View

16'

24'

Varies with house dimensions

6'

Footing and Framing Plan

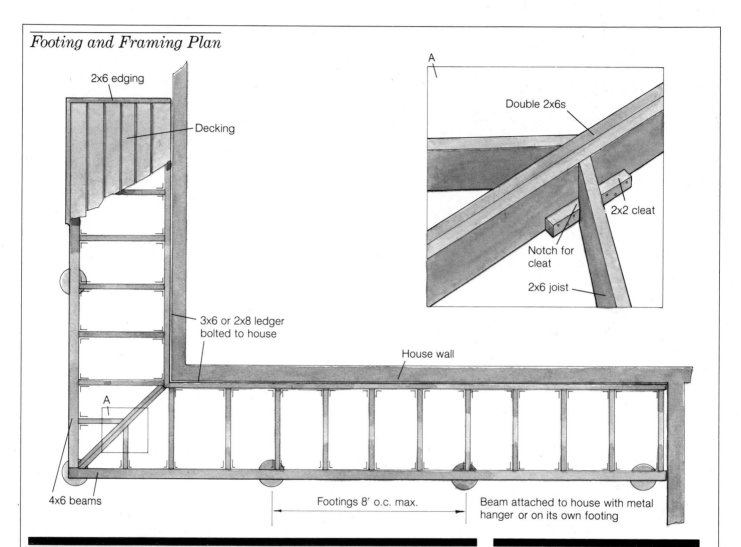

2x6 edging

Decking

A

Double 2x6s

2x2 cleat

Notch for cleat

2x6 joist

3x6 or 2x8 ledger bolted to house

House wall

A

4x6 beams

Footings 8' o.c. max.

Beam attached to house with metal hanger or on its own footing

Materials List

Footings	15 cu ft concrete {for 6 piers (8"x8"x8") and footings (18"x18"x12")}			
	6 metal post anchors			
	12 $^3/_8$"x4$^1/_2$" carriage bolts with nuts and washers			
Framing	Posts	4x4s	1	6' length (for 6 short posts; lengths vary)
	Ledgers	2x8s	1	18' length; 1 10' length
	Beams	4x6s	1	24' length; 1 16' length
	Joists	2x6s	11	12' lengths
	Joist hangers	2x6s	38	
	Beam hanger	4x6s	1	
	Bolts		20	$^3/_8$" dia lag or machine bolts for ledger (size varies with thickness of siding)
			100	$^3/_8$" washers (extras are for spacers)
Decking		2x6s	408 lineal feet (204 sq ft)	
Nails		5#	joist hanger nails	
		8#	12d HDG common	
		3#	16d HDG common	

Construction Techniques

This design is intended for homes with a wood floor from 12 to 18 inches above grade, such as homes built over a crawlspace or basement. If your floor is higher, you can raise the deck by resting the joists on top of the beam. The resulting overhang makes it easier to conceal the footings. You could also raise the deck by lengthening the posts. However, if the deck is higher than 24 inches it starts feeling like a balcony and needs a railing.

Because the deck is attached to the house, it is very important to maintain required clearances between earth and wood, usually 8 inches. It is also advisable to use all pressure-treated or naturally durable lumber.

Site Preparation

Be sure the ground slopes away from the house at least ½ inch per foot and that any downspouts in the area of the deck have leaders to carry the water beyond the perimeter of the deck. Provide for weed control with chemical retardants or a polyethylene sheet covered with rocks or gravel.

The house itself, where the new deck is attached, should be in sound condition. Repair any damaged siding and paint any new wood.

Layout and Footings

The side of the house provides an easy control line for laying out the deck. When you excavate for the footings and are digging near the foundation, be careful not to disturb plumbing lines, drain tiles, or other utility lines. Plan the placement of the piers so their outside edge is flush with the outside edge of the beam. This way you can conceal them more easily using a fascia board or plantings. If the beam will be resting directly on the piers, level all the piers to each other.

Ledger, Beam, and Joists

The ledger should be 3-by lumber if it is available; otherwise, use 2-by that is one size larger than the joists. To attach the ledger to the house, measure 2½ inches down from the floor level and draw a level line along the siding of the house, using a long level or a straightedge and short level. This mark represents the top of the ledger. It allows for a 1-inch drop from floor level to the top of the deck boards. This drop prevents water or melting snow from backing up into the house.

Bolt the ledger to the floor framing of the house, using zinc-coated lag bolts or carriage bolts. See page 45 for specific bolting techniques.

Install the beams and joists as described on page 33. At the point where the two beams intersect over one pier, use a miter joint. Where the end of one beam abuts the house, attach it to the house with a wide joist hanger or provide a footing and pier.

Framing Detail

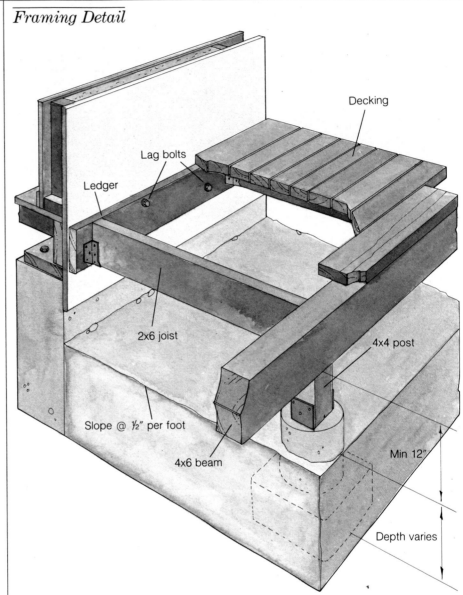

Decking

Lag bolts

Ledger

2x6 joist

Slope @ ½" per foot

4x6 beam

4x4 post

Min 12"

Depth varies

Decking and Fascia

The deck boards for this engawa are 2 by 6s, but wider ones may be used. When installing deck boards that are 2 by 6 or wider, take the following precautions to minimize cupping. First, lay the boards bark side up. Second, use three nails at each joist, setting the outside two at opposite angles. Finally, as insurance, you may want to cut saw kerfs up the middle of the bottom of each board before installing it to minimize cupping. Make the cuts ½ inch deep (maximum) along the entire length of the board.

For a cleaner profile, install a 2 by 8 fascia board flush with the top of the decking. However, since no ends are visible, you may leave the decking without a fascia.

At the corner where the deck changes direction, use a miter joint, or you can run the decking boards along one of the walls all the way out to the edge of the intersecting section of deck. The deck boards of the other deck arm would then butt against the first board of the original layout. Such a corner would not require a diagonal joist.

Bolting a Ledger to a House

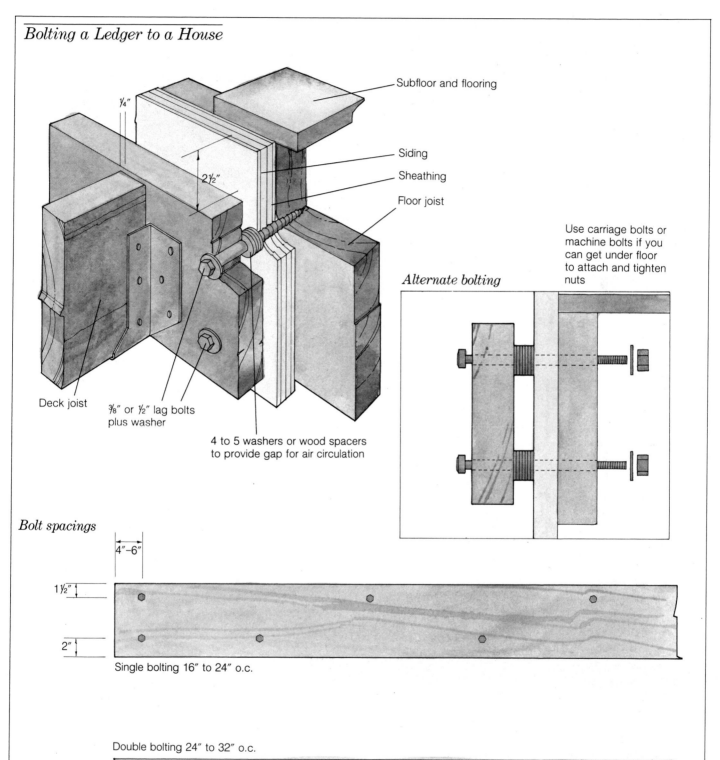

Subfloor and flooring

Siding

Sheathing

Floor joist

1/4"

2 1/2"

Deck joist

3/8" or 1/2" lag bolts plus washer

4 to 5 washers or wood spacers to provide gap for air circulation

Alternate bolting

Use carriage bolts or machine bolts if you can get under floor to attach and tighten nuts

Bolt spacings

4"–6"

1 1/2"

2"

Single bolting 16" to 24" o.c.

Double bolting 24" to 32" o.c.

PLAN 8
Stepped Platforms with an Angle

For a home with a sloping yard or with a first floor that is too high for a single, low platform, the answer is a multilevel deck that hugs the ground but allows a smooth transition between the house and yard.

This design features three platforms that create a cascade effect from the house to a yard that slopes away from it. Because the height of this deck averages 20 to 30 inches above grade, it does not require railings, but it does use benches to provide closure and to define spaces.

One obvious distinction of this deck design is its angled lower platform. Angles can be an interesting and dramatic design feature for

decks, but their use should be governed by a few basic principles. First, they should have a purpose. Second, angles should be aligned with prominent architectural or visual axes. Finally, all the angles should be in the same family, in this case, 130, 40, and 90 degrees.

Construction Techniques

The deck in this plan has two main platforms separated by one step and a pair of long platform steps to the house. The number of footings is kept to a minimum by using a beam-and-joist system throughout and by using

one of the beams to help support both main platforms. Neither of the main platforms is actually attached to the house, so the plan could easily be used for a freestanding deck by eliminating the steps to the house.

The deck is intended for a gently sloping site or for a level site where the floor of the house is approximately 36 to 42 inches above grade. For steeper slopes, you could shorten all the deck dimensions or increase the number of connecting steps to keep the deck within 30 inches of grade on the downhill side. It is also possible to increase or decrease the number of steps to the house without altering the basic structure.

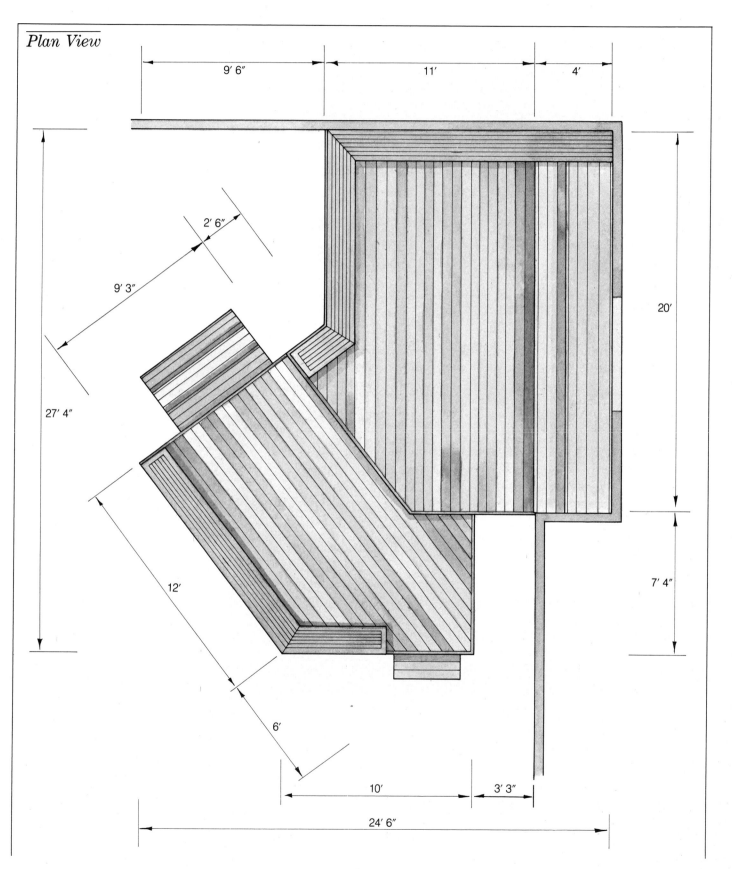

9′ 6″

11′

4′

2′ 6″

9′ 3″

20′

27′ 4″

7′ 4″

12′

6′

10′

3′ 3″

24′ 6″

Layout and Footings

To locate the footings, use dimensions on the framing diagram and standard layout techniques. To find the 130-degree angle where the two decks join and where the bench of the lower deck bends, use either a transit or the variant of the carpenter's 3-4-5 triangle. In this case, the variant would be 6-8-12³/₄ (see illustration).

The footings are round piers, 8 to 12 inches in diameter, formed on site with fiber tubes. Their exact diameter and depth will vary with local conditions, as well as with the size of the footing at the bottom of each pier. Note that the pier that supports the intersection of two beams should be large enough for a 4-by-8 post.

Ledger

The ledger for the steps to the house supports the joists for the bottom step. If there are two steps, as shown in this plan, locate the top of the joist for the bottom step 10 inches below floor level. This allows for 1¹/₂-inch-thick decking on both steps and a 1-inch drop between the ledger and the top step. If there is only one step, place the top of the ledger 2¹/₂ inches below floor level. If there are three steps, place the top of the ledger 2¹/₂ inches below floor level and use cut-out stringers for the stair framing.

Posts, Beams, and Joists

The lengths of the posts will depend on the slope and the height of the piers. A critical and difficult process for decks of this size is leveling each post, especially when the deck has different levels itself. Use the ledger board as a control point and calculate the distance below that point for the top of each post by consulting the elevation drawing on page 50. Then use a transit, line level, or hydrolevel to transfer that dimension to the post and mark it for cutting.

After you have all the posts, install all the beams, starting with the lower deck. Then trim the beam ends. Next, install the joists and rim joists, again starting with the lower platform.

Decking and Fascia

Use standard techniques for nailing the deck boards, trimming their ends, and attaching fascia boards. Use specialized tools for miter cuts and marking proper angles—an angle divider or various protractor squares.

You can also lay a protractor over the actual corner, divide the angle in half, and mark this angle on the board. Marking the board or setting the same angle on a power saw is easier with a bevel gauge. Otherwise, use the protractor to lay out the board and adjust the saw blade if the saw does not have calibrated markings accurate enough to read.

Materials List

Footings			1 cu yd concrete for 11 piers (8"x8"x8") and footing (18"x18"x12")
			40 lineal feet #4 rebar (cut into 18" pieces)
			11 metal post anchors
			22 ³/₈"x4¹/₂" carriage bolts with nuts and washers
Framing	Ledger	2x8s	1 20' length
	Posts	4x4s	(number and length vary with site)
		4x8s	2 (length varies with site)
	Beams	4x8s	1 12' length; 2 14' lengths; 1 18' length; 1 20' length
	Joists	2x8s	8 8' lengths; 1 10' length; 8 12' lengths; 2 14' lengths
		2x6s	1 8' length; 7 10' lengths; 10 12' lengths; 1 20' length
	Blocking	2x8s	1 18' length (cut into 2 ± pieces)
		2x6s	1 14' length (cut into 2 ± pieces)
	Joist hangers	2x6s	7
		2x8s	11
	Bolts		15 ³/₈" dia lag bolts with washers, or machine bolts with washers and nuts
			75 ³/₈" washers
			6 ³/₈"x4" carriage bolts
			2 ⁵/₈"x10" carriage bolts
Decking		2x6s	916 lineal feet (440 sq ft)
Fascia		2x4s	2 8' lengths; 2 10' lengths; 2 12' lengths; 1 14' length; 2 20' lengths
Bench	Uprights	2x12s	3 10' lengths (cut into 24 14¹/₂" pieces)
	Cleats	2x4s	2 12' lengths (cut into 24 13" pieces)
	Stringers	2x4s	3 6' lengths; 2 10' lengths; 2 12' lengths; 1 14' length; 1 16' length
	Seat	2x4s	4 10' lengths; 7 12' lengths; 2 14' lengths; 2 16' lengths
		2x2s	240 lineal feet
Stairs	Stringer	2x12s	1 12' length
	Treads	2x6s	3 12' lengths
		2x4s	1 18' length
Nails		3#	joist hanger nails
		30#	12 HDG common
		25#	16d HDG common

Footing and Framing Plan

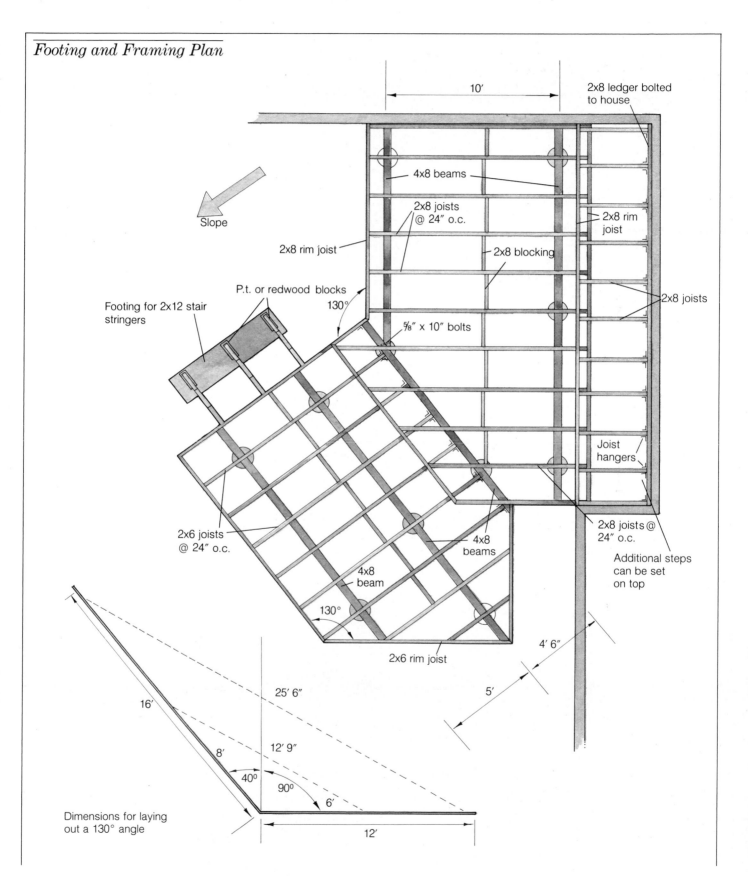

10'

2x8 ledger bolted to house

4x8 beams

Slope

2x8 joists @ 24" o.c.

2x8 rim joist

2x8 rim joist

2x8 blocking

2x8 joists

Footing for 2x12 stair stringers

P.t. or redwood blocks

130°

⅝" x 10" bolts

2x6 joists @ 24" o.c.

4x8 beams

Joist hangers

4x8 beam

130°

2x8 joists @ 24" o.c.

Additional steps can be set on top

2x6 rim joist

4' 6"

25' 6"

5'

16'

12' 9"

8'

40°

90°

6'

Dimensions for laying out a 130° angle

12'

49

PLAN 8

Access Stairs
Build stairs to the garden after the deck is finished. For one or two steps, build simple platforms as described on page 86. For a longer staircase, use techniques described in the Ortho book *Basic Carpentry Techniques*. It is important that all the risers be the same height, preferably the 7½ inches used throughout the deck. The actual number of steps and precise dimensions for each step will depend on site conditions.

Benches
Many bench styles would look quite handsome on this deck because the benches follow the dramatic angles of the deck itself, and even "skate" over one of the steps. The design suggested with this plan was chosen because it can be built after the deck is finished and because its simple 2 by 12 legs are easy to attach to the decking and present a very thin profile when viewed straight ahead. See pages 84-85 for other bench ideas.

Unlike smaller benches, which can be prefabricated and then installed, this bench is too large to build separately. It must be built from the ground up. Start by attaching the 2 by 4 cleats to all the uprights, making sure all dimensions are accurate.

Then toenail the uprights to the decking. Predrill the uprights for each nail in order to prevent splitting, and set the nails carefully for a neater appearance. To make sure the upright is aligned properly, hold a carpenter's square against it and the back edge of the deck before you nail it.

After the uprights are in place, nail the 2 by 4s and 2 by 2s to the cleats. Use nails to space the gaps evenly, and blind-nail the 2 by 2s. Make all joints over cleats. Miter the joints at the corners, using the angle-cutting techniques described above for fascia boards. If you want to add fascia boards to the benches, you can use a 2 by 4, as shown, or nailed so its top is flush with the bench surface. You can also use a 1 by 4 nailed below the decking. You must choose the style you prefer before you nail down the bench decking, since the 1 by 4 style requires the decking to overhang the cleats by 1½ inches and the 2 by 4 style requires it to be flush.

Framing Detail
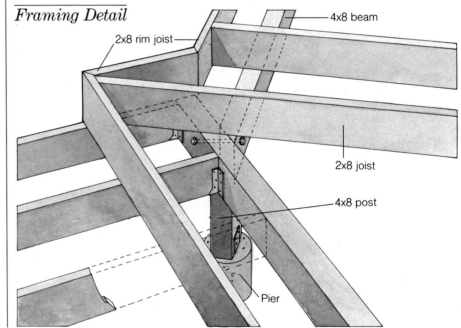

Section
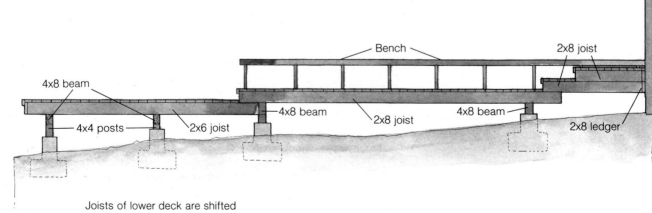

Joints of lower deck are shifted 130° from the upper joists

Stair and Bench Details

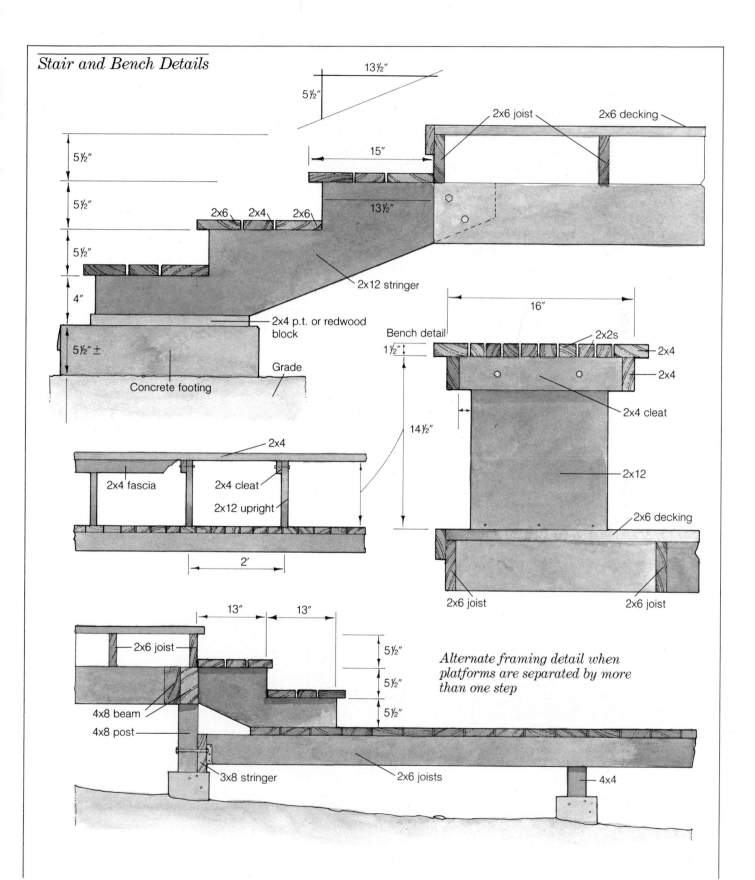

13½"

5½"

5½"

5½"

5½"

4"

5½"±

15"

13½"

2x6 joist   2x6 decking

2x6   2x4   2x6

2x12 stringer

2x4 p.t. or redwood block

Grade

Concrete footing

Bench detail

16"

1½"

14½"

2x2s

2x4

2x4

2x4 cleat

2x12

2x6 decking

2x6 joist   2x6 joist

2x4

2x4 fascia   2x4 cleat

2x12 upright

2'

13"   13"

5½"

5½"

5½"

2x6 joist

Alternate framing detail when platforms are separated by more than one step

4x8 beam

4x8 post

3x8 stringer

2x6 joists

4x4

PLAN 9
A Wraparound Entry Deck

This deck is actually a simple one-step platform wrapped around a corner of the house, but its most noticeable feature is the solid railing that extends to the ground. It shows how a deck addition can look like an original part of the house.

In this example the railing matches the house's siding. Because this deck also serves as a front entry, the siding serves other functions besides dressing up the deck: it creates privacy and seclusion, blocks noise, and even creates a sense of anticipation to those entering the home.

The two levels of this deck help to define activity spaces and create visual interest. Changing the direction of the decking boards makes the single step easier to see. This deck could be simplified by making it all the same level, with deck boards running the same way.

Plan View

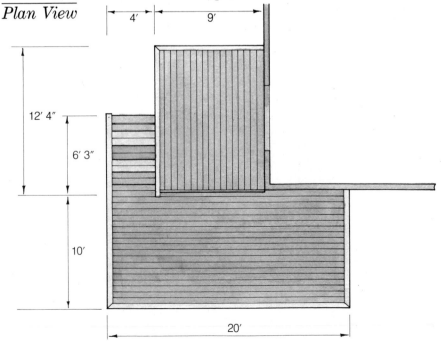

4' 9'

12' 4"

6' 3"

10'

20'

Structural Features

This deck has three design elements that require special structural features. Wherever the deck meets the house, it needs the support of ledger boards. For safety, the one-step change in levels needs to be visible. This requires a joist system that allows the decking boards to change direction at the step. The siding for the railing and skirts requires continuous support from the ground to the railing top. Therefore, the framing for this deck places the posts outside the stringers and joists. The siding is attached to these posts.

Construction Techniques

Layout and Footings

To lay out the footing locations, use the dimensions specified on the framing plan and decking diagram. Because all posts are placed at the perimeter of the deck, you can use the exact dimensions of the deck. Run string lines at these points to represent their outside edges.

This deck requires care in forming the footings. In order to frame up studs and plates for the siding, the tops of the piers need to be level. If the integrity of the design requires you to drop the siding below the tops of the piers, you can form the outside face of each pier so that it will be flush with the face of the post. However, this procedure affects the strength of the piers and brings the siding below recommended earthwood clearances (which may not pertain if the siding is pressure-treated). If you want to do this, get help from the local building department or from a professional builder or designer.

Aside from these issues, the footings and piers follow typical construction techniques for decks. Their depth and style depend on local conditions. In some areas you can even forego concrete piers and bury posts directly in the ground, but use posts treated for ground contact.

Ledgers, Posts, and Stringers

Mark the ledger locations $2\frac{1}{2}$ inches below floor level at the doorway. Note that the ledgers are at different levels, separated by a vertical distance of $7\frac{1}{2}$ inches.

Bolt the upper ledger to the house first. The lower ledger consists of a single 2 by 10 bolted to the house and a double 2 by 10 that extends beyond the house. Before installing the double ledger, measure and mark its length from the corner of the house to the end of the extension. Cut both 2 by 10s to length, and nail them together, 16 inches on center. Then erect the far post and connect the stringer to the posts.

Materials List

Footings		1.25 cu yd concrete for 12 piers (8"x8"x8") and footings (18"x18"x12")	
		13 metal post anchors	
		26 ⅜"x4½" carriage bolts with nuts and washers	
Stair Landing		.25 cu yd concrete (7 cu ft) for 54"x36"x6" slab	
		2 anchor bolts for 2x4 cleat	
Framing	Posts	4x4s	15 8' lengths
	Ledgers	2x10s	1 12' length; 1 14' length; 1 20' length
	Stringers or	2x8s 3x8s	2 12' lengths; 2 20' lengths 1 12' length; 1 20' length
	Joists	2x8s	18 10' lengths
	Blocking	2x8s	2 10' lengths; 1 12' length
	Stairs	2x12s	3 12' lengths
		2x4s	1 4' length pressure-treated
	Ledger bolts		12 ⅜" dia lag or machine bolts + 60 washers
	Post bolts		8 ⅜" dia lag bolts and washers
	Stringer bolts		16 ⅜"x7" carriage bolts with nuts and washers
			10 ⅜"x6" carriage bolts with nuts and washers
			2 ½"x11" carriage bolts with nuts and washers
	Joist hangers	2x8s	39
Decking		2x6s	18 12' lengths; 20 20' lengths (310 sq ft)
Stair Treads		2x6s	4 10' lengths (for 5 steps)
		2x2s	2 10' lengths (for 5 steps)
Railing and Skirts		(68 lineal feet)	
	Frame	2x4s	27 8' lengths; 5 10' lengths; 2 12' lengths; 1 16' length; 2 20' lengths
	Cap rail	2x6s	1 8' length; 3 10' lengths; 1 12' length; 1 20' length
	Siding		Sheathing and/or siding material to cover 700 sq ft (460 on outside of deck, 210 on inside of railings + 5% waste)
	Trim	1x4s	2 8' lengths; 6 10' lengths; 2 12' lengths; 2 20' lengths
	Moisture membrane		68 lineal feet of sheet metal cap or 6" wide 30# felt
Nails		5#	joist hanger
		17#	12d HDG common
		15#	16d HDG common
	Nails		for siding and/or sheathing, depending on material used

PLAN 9

Next, erect all the rest of the posts and hold them in plumb position with temporary diagonal bracing. Do not try to cut the posts to exact height until the deck platform is finished. Then mark each post so its top will be level with the top of the ledger (or ledger line) opposite it. Temporarily nail the stringer so its top is flush with the mark on each post. Then drill holes and bolt. If the stringer consists of double 2 by 8s instead of a 3 by 8, be sure both 2 by 8s are made of pressure-treated lumber.

Joists and Decking

Install joists 24 inches on center. (See page 30 for typical techniques for joist hangers.) The layout will leave one odd-sized spacing, which should be at either end. Install blocking for both levels.

Install the deck boards so their edges are flush against the posts. The cavities between the posts do not need decking because they will be enclosed by the solid siding. Trim the single step with 2 by 4 fascia.

Section Through Both Platforms

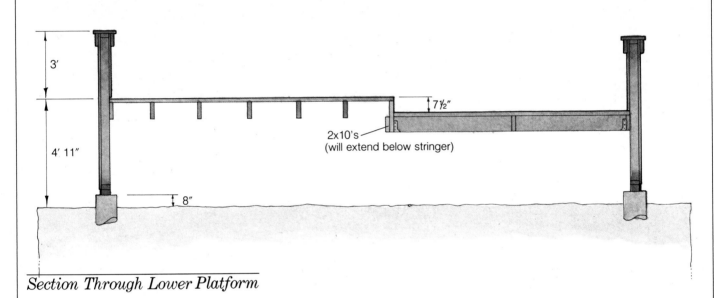

3′

4′ 11″

7½″

2x10's
(will extend below stringer)

8″

Section Through Lower Platform

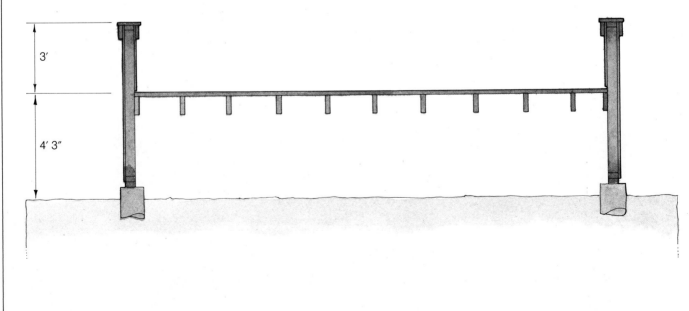

3′

4′ 3″

Footing and Framing Plan

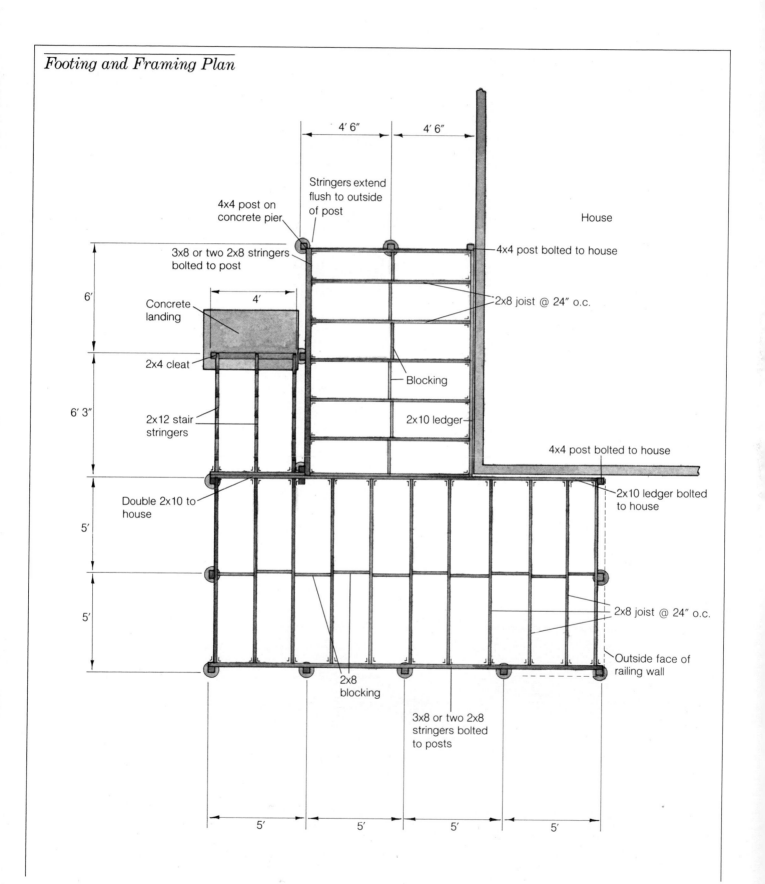

4' 6"
4' 6"

Stringers extend flush to outside of post

House

4x4 post on concrete pier

3x8 or two 2x8 stringers bolted to post

4x4 post bolted to house

6'

Concrete landing

4'

2x8 joist @ 24" o.c.

2x4 cleat

Blocking

6' 3"

2x12 stair stringers

2x10 ledger

4x4 post bolted to house

Double 2x10 to house

2x10 ledger bolted to house

5'

5'

2x8 joist @ 24" o.c.

5'

2x8 blocking

Outside face of railing wall

3x8 or two 2x8 stringers bolted to posts

5'
5'
5'
5'

Stairs

You can terminate stairs at the bottom in several ways, but this plan uses a concrete landing because it is a front entry. You can pour the landing when you pour the footings. Insert anchor bolts for the 2 by 4 cleat while the concrete is wet.

Three 2 by 12 cutout stringers support the stairs. Make the tread cutout 11½ inches wide and calculate the riser cutout by dividing the total rise of the stairs by the number of risers (see Ortho's books *How to Design & Build Decks & Patios* and *Basic Carpentry Techniques* for stair-building information). In this plan the risers are 7½ inches.

Attach the top of the stringers to the double 2 by 12 header with joist hangers. To attach the stringers to the landing, notch their bottoms and fit them over the 2 by 4 cleat. Toenail the stringers into the cleat with 8d or 12d nails. If the stringers are not made of pressure-treated or naturally durable lumber, they should not make direct contact with the concrete. Instead, install 2 by 4 blocks of pressure-treated or decay-resistant lumber on the concrete and trim the bottoms of the stringers to compensate for the height of the blocks. Toenail stringers to the blocks.

Framing Detail

½" x 12"
carriage bolts

To pier

Stair Detail

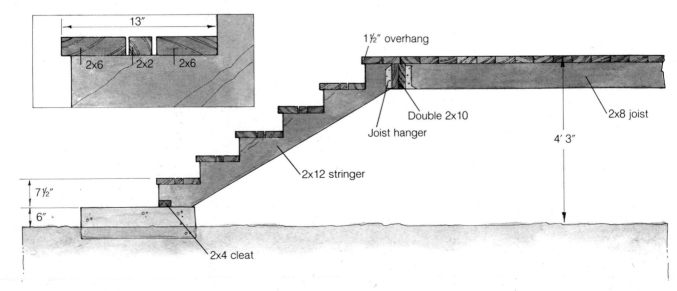

13"

2x6   2x2   2x6

1½" overhang

Double 2x10

Joist hanger

2x8 joist

2x12 stringer

4' 3"

7½"

6"

2x4 cleat

Make the treads for this stairway with two 2 by 6s separated by a 2 by 2. The nosings should overhang by 1½ inches. The top step is actually a continuation of the lower deck's decking boards. You will find it easier to install the treads after the siding is in place. Leave a ¼-inch gap between the end of each tread and the siding for air circulation and moisture control.

Railings and Skirts

This plan uses solid railings that match the house siding. The railings also extend to the ground on the outside of the deck.

First, cut the posts to length: 33 inches above the decking for 36-inch railings. Then nail a 2 by 4 over the tops of the posts, and 2 by 4 plates between the posts just above the footings. The plates are easier to install if you use metal connectors, such as fence framing clips. They are nailed to the posts and have pockets for holding the ends of the plates. If you do not use framing clips, toenail each end of the plate into the post with four 8d galvanized nails. Then measure and cut vertical studs to fit between the bottom plate and the 2 by 4 cap. Nail them in place, 16 inches on center, and toenail them to the stringers as well.

Nail sheathing or siding to the framework in the same way you would apply exterior siding (although building paper is not necessary). If you're using shingles, shakes, or stucco, you should install CDX or similar plywood sheathing first. Install horizontal wood siding or plywood siding directly to the studs.

After the siding or sheathing is installed, you can trim the top of the railing with a 2 by 8 cap and 1 by 4 trim on the side. To prevent moisture from leaking to the inside of the railing, place 15-pound felt over the top plate or have a sheet-metal shop make a sheet-metal cap to fit over the assembly. Then install the 2 by 8 cap and 1 by 4 trim.

Railing Detail

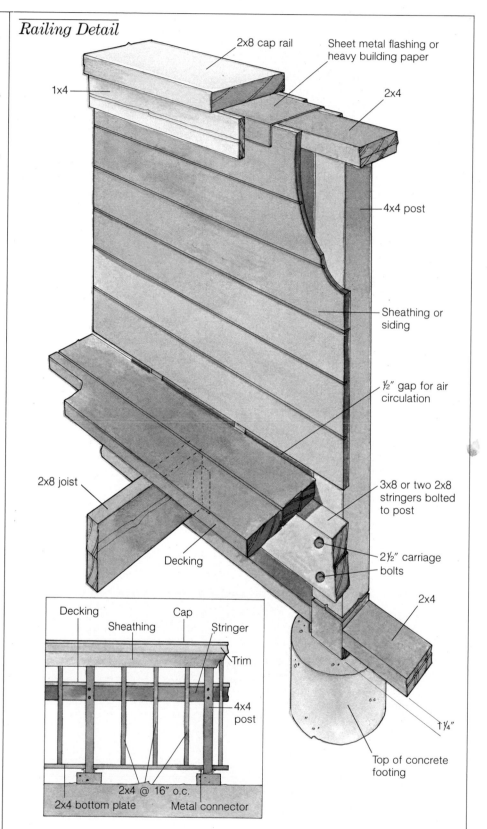

2x8 cap rail

Sheet metal flashing or heavy building paper

1x4

2x4

4x4 post

Sheathing or siding

½" gap for air circulation

2x8 joist

Decking

3x8 or two 2x8 stringers bolted to post

2½" carriage bolts

2x4

Top of concrete footing

1¼"

Decking

Cap

Sheathing

Stringer

Trim

4x4 post

2x4 @ 16" o.c.

2x4 bottom plate

Metal connector

PLAN 10
A Split-Level Deck with a View

This deck consists of two platforms with a vertical separation of 3 feet. The separation allows the upper platform to remain at the same level as the floor, while bringing the lower platform closer to the yard. Such an arrangement may be desirable when the ground slopes away from the house or when the landscaping is natural and invites observation.

Separating the platforms by 3 feet or more also creates an interesting interaction between them. The upper platform feels like an observation deck that oversees activity in the lower area, and the lower deck has a magnetic quality that invites closer exploration. This difference between the two levels creates a dynamic and versatile space.

The shape of the deck has a number of advantages. If the house shades a potential deck site, this deck may extend far enough outward to capture precious sunlight. The upper platform is wide enough for a comfortable seating area but narrow enough for easy access to the lower deck. The lower platform has two points that thrust into the yard, somewhat like a ship's prow. Each creates a strong visual axis toward a potential focal point or view corridor. These aesthetic features create a deck that is dynamic and exhilarating, that invites exploration, and that pulls the outdoors and indoors together in a stimulating way.

Plan View

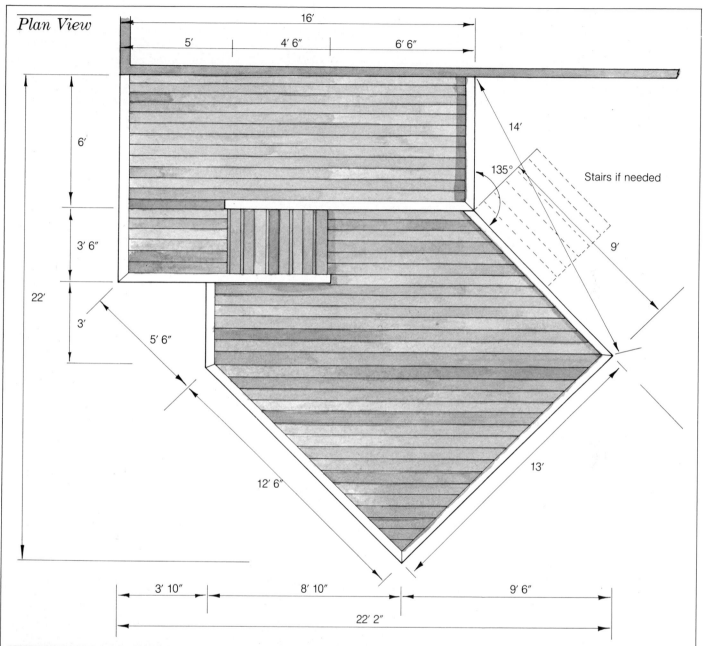

Structural Features

This design uses stringers throughout the deck, rather than beams. They enable the two platforms to share common posts. They also keep the perimeter posts on the outside of the deck so they can support a solid railing system without any interference from other structural members.

Another feature is the use of angles, in this case 45, 90, and 135 degrees. The deck could be built with other angles, such as all 90 degrees, with basically the same structural system.

Construction Techniques

Layout and Footings

The outside edges of the posts correspond to the perimeter dimensions of the deck, so most of the layout is fairly simple. The main "bend" in the deck consists of a 135-degree angle, which is formed by a triangle whose sides are 6 feet, 9 feet, and 14 feet.

Because the stringers intersect from two different directions, you must position footings precisely. Three posts carry stringers from both decks. When setting metal anchor brackets, be sure to align them for the 4-inch dimension of the 4 by 6 posts. If you turn the bracket the wrong way, the post will not fit into the bracket in the proper direction.

PLAN 10

Ledgers and Posts

Attach the 2 by 8 ledger to the house, following the procedures outlined on page 44. Use it as a reference for marking posts for the stringers, after the posts are erected and braced.

Install posts and stringers for the upper deck first, so you can make reliable measurements from them for the lower deck. When they are in

place, measure down 36 inches along the 4 by 6 posts, from the top of the upper deck's 2 by 8 stringer. This measurement represents the top of the lower deck's 2 by 8 stringers. The top of the 3 by 8 (or doubled 2 by 8) perimeter stringer is 36 inches from the upper deck's stringer. Using a line level, hydrolevel, or long straightedge and hand level, transfer these marks to the other posts for the lower deck.

When the posts are marked, install the stringers. Where they attach to the 4 by 6 posts, you will have to cut notches so the stringers maintain a 3½-inch separation and also have a flat surface to be bolted against. Attach all stringers with ½-inch-diameter carriage or machine bolts. Any doubled-up stringers should be made of pressure-treated lumber.

Section Showing Both Platforms

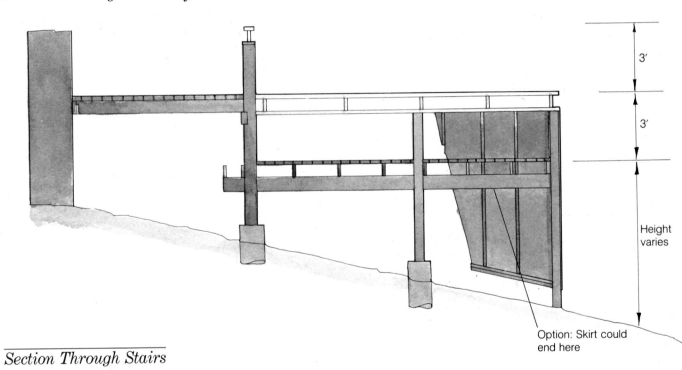

3'

3'

Height varies

Option: Skirt could end here

Section Through Stairs

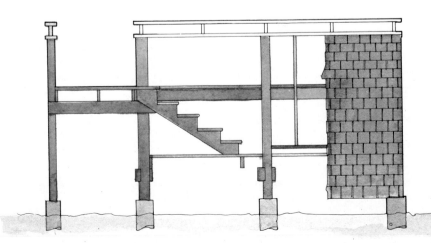

Post and Framing Plan

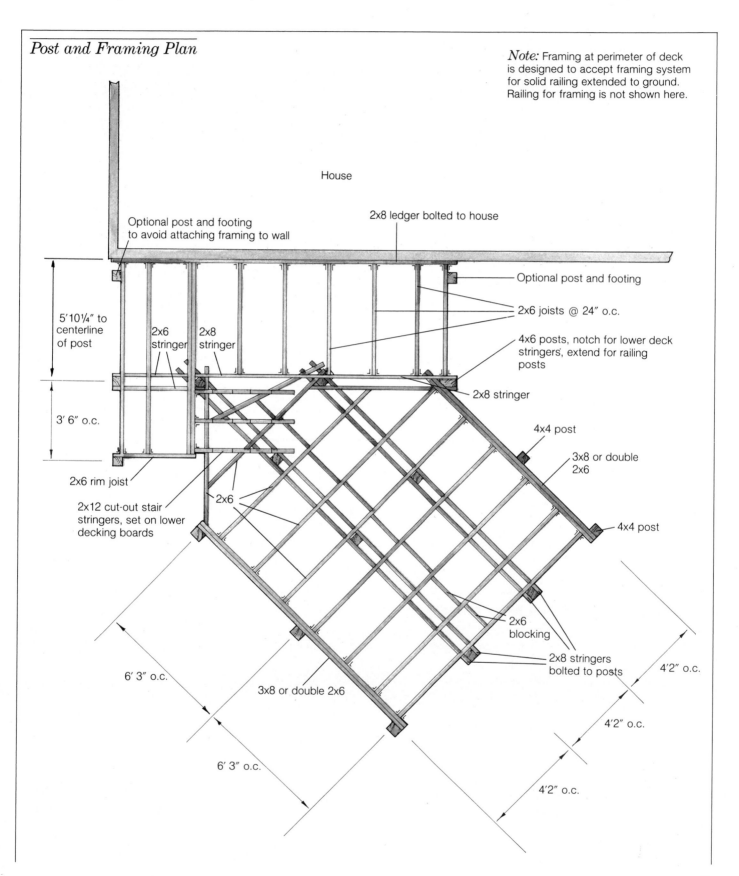

Note: Framing at perimeter of deck is designed to accept framing system for solid railing extended to ground. Railing for framing is not shown here.

House

Optional post and footing to avoid attaching framing to wall

2x8 ledger bolted to house

Optional post and footing

5' 10¼" to centerline of post

2x6 stringer

2x8 stringer

2x6 joists @ 24" o.c.

4x6 posts, notch for lower deck stringers, extend for railing posts

2x8 stringer

3' 6" o.c.

4x4 post

3x8 or double 2x6

2x6 rim joist

4x4 post

2x12 cut-out stair stringers, set on lower decking boards

2x6

2x6 blocking

2x8 stringers bolted to posts

6' 3" o.c.

4' 2" o.c.

3x8 or double 2x6

4' 2" o.c.

6' 3" o.c.

4' 2" o.c.

PLAN 10

Stringers and Joists

Install joists for the upper deck by attaching them to the ledger with joist hangers. For most of the joists, the opposite end is also attached by joist hangers. The best method is to nail one joist hanger to the ledger and the other to one end of the joist. Use a special double joist hanger for the 4 by 6 (or double 2 by 6s).

Install joists for the lower deck with joist hangers at their ends and toenailing into the center stringers. The short joists near the stairs have beveled ends, which you can mark by positioning the joist over its location and scribing the bottom of it where it meets the intersecting joist.

Decking

Nail the decking so its edges will be flush with the inside edges of the posts. You may need to trim the tops of the two interior posts of the lower deck so the decking boards will clear. Be sure to cut the tops at an angle (approximately 30 degrees) for water runoff. The third interior post will be a railing post for the stairs. Fit decking around it.

Stairs

If the distance between deck surfaces is exactly 36 inches, the riser dimension for the stair stringers will be $7^3/_{16}$ inches. The treads, then, will be $11^1/_2$ inches (cutout dimension; the actual tread material will be 13 inches). Cut out three 2 by 12 stringers. Attach them to the 4 by 6 header with joist hangers and to the decking with toenailing.

See the illustration for the tread dimensions, which uses 2 by 6 and 2 by 2 tread stock. The topmost step is actually an extension of the upper decking. Since this decking is perpendicular to the steps, you can wait to install it until the stair framing is finished, or make the topmost tread the same as the rest of the steps. If you run the upper decking to the nose of the first step, you will have to support it with a 2 by 8 riser. Attach risers to all the steps for a more finished look.

Railings

The railing system for this deck is the same as that for Plan 8. Since this example has wood shingles, you would need to install $1/2$-inch pressure-treated CDX plywood first. Then install the shingles, a sheet-metal cap, the 1 by 4 trim (or smaller, if desired), and the 2 by 8 railing cap. The siding should be finished before treads are installed on the stairs.

Notice that the siding does not have to extend all the way to the ground in this example, since the natural setting does not make it necessary. Where a more finished look is required, you can use the techniques of Plan 8 for extending siding down to the footings, or even below.

Materials List

Footings		1.6 cu yd concrete for 17 piers (8"x8"x8") and footings (18"x18"x12")							
		17 metal post anchors							
		34 $^3/_8$"x$4^1/_2$" carriage bolts with nuts and washers							
Framing	Posts	4x4s	11	8' lengths;	1	12' length (varies with site)			
		4x6s	3	8' lengths (varies with site)					
	Ledger	2x8s	1	16' length					
	Stringers	2x8s	1	12' length;	2	16' lengths;	2	18' lengths;	
		2x6s	1	8' length;	2	12' lengths;	2	14' lengths;	
	or	3x8s	1	14' length;	1	16' length			
	Joists	2x6s	1	8' length;	8	10' lengths;	8	12' lengths	
	Blocking	2x6s	1	14' length					
	Stair stringer	2x12s	3	8' lengths					
	Joist hangers	2x6s	29;	2x8s	3;	3x6s	1		
	Ledger bolts		12	$^3/_8$"x5" lag nuts and 60 washers					
	Stringer bolts		28	$^3/_8$"x7" carriage bolts with nuts					
			6	$^3/_8$"x6" carriage bolts with nuts					
Decking		2x6s	620 lineal feet (288 sq ft)						
Stair Treads		2x6s	8	4' lengths					
		2x2s	4	4' lengths					
Railing and Skirts		(80 lineal feet of railing; assumes skirt extends to ground)							
	Frame	2x4s	22	8' lengths;	6	10' lengths;			
			5	12' lengths;	9	14' lengths			
	Siding	Sheathing and/or siding material to cover 800 sq ft (568 on outside of deck, 216 on inside of railing + 2% waste)							
	Moisture membrane	80 lineal feet of sheet metal cap or 6" wide 30# felt							
	Railing	2x6s	6	10' lengths;	4	12' lengths;			
			4	16' lengths					
Nails		5#	joist hanger nails						
		15#	12d HDG common						
		15#	16d HDG common						
		Nails for sheathing/siding, depending on material used							

Detail for Cutting Post Tops

Cut tops of interior post at 30° angles for water runoff.

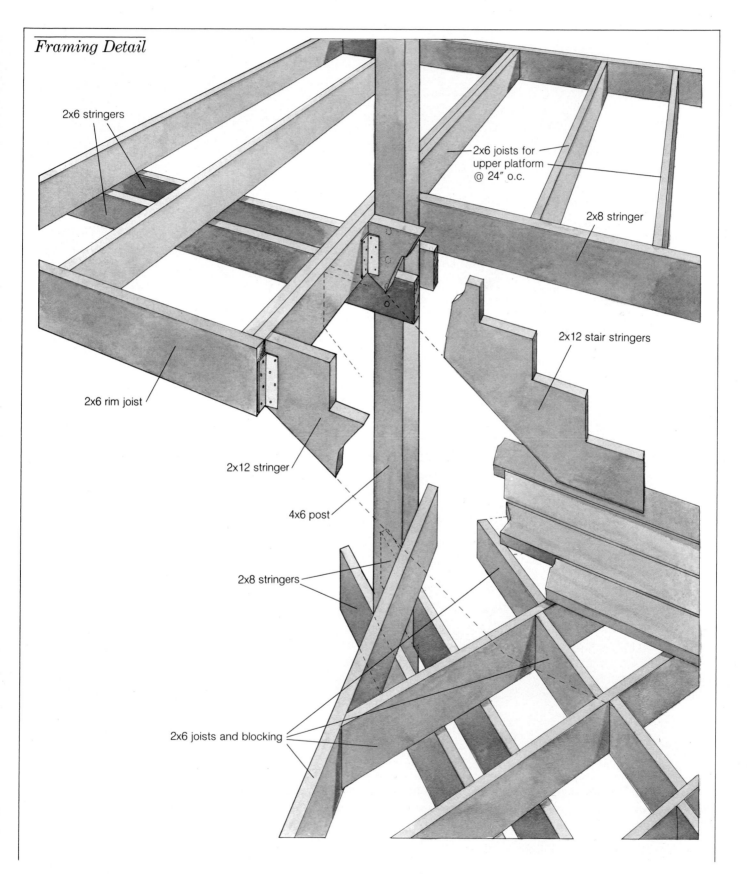

Framing Detail

2x6 stringers

2x6 joists for
upper platform
@ 24" o.c.

2x8 stringer

2x12 stair stringers

2x6 rim joist

2x12 stringer

4x6 post

2x8 stringers

2x6 joists and blocking

PLAN 11
A Multilevel Cascade

If this plan looks familiar, it's because the deck is featured on the cover of Ortho's book *How to Design & Build Decks & Patios.* This seemingly complex and enormous deck is really a series of platforms, connected by stairways and steps, that cascade down a steep slope. It also wraps around one corner of the house and provides an outdoor connection between the upper and lower floors.

Such a deck offers a dramatic setting for many outdoor activities. It creates a dynamic interaction both between the outdoor and indoor spaces, and among its own various levels. It tames a steep slope. It is expansive enough to offer either shade or full sun, areas for sitting or for movement, distant views or nearby sights, privacy or exposure—all at the same time.

Although this particular site is sloped, the deck could be adapted for a split-level home or a two-story home on a level site. It solves many of the problems created by an ordinary high-level deck. One is the isolation of such a deck from the ground. This design creates an inviting connection through the use of intermediate platforms. Another problem of high decks is that they often overshadow and darken the rooms below. The downstairs windows of this home still have sunlight and views because the deck extends out away from the house. Finally, a high-level deck can look ''stuck on'' unless it blends with the house. In this design the deck is bold and has an architectural feel, but blends into the forest setting as well as balances the size of the house.

Structural Features

The deck system consists of four platforms, two stairways of equal length (8 treads, 9 risers each), and an intermediate step between the two lower levels. Two of the platforms are attached to the house and two are freestanding.

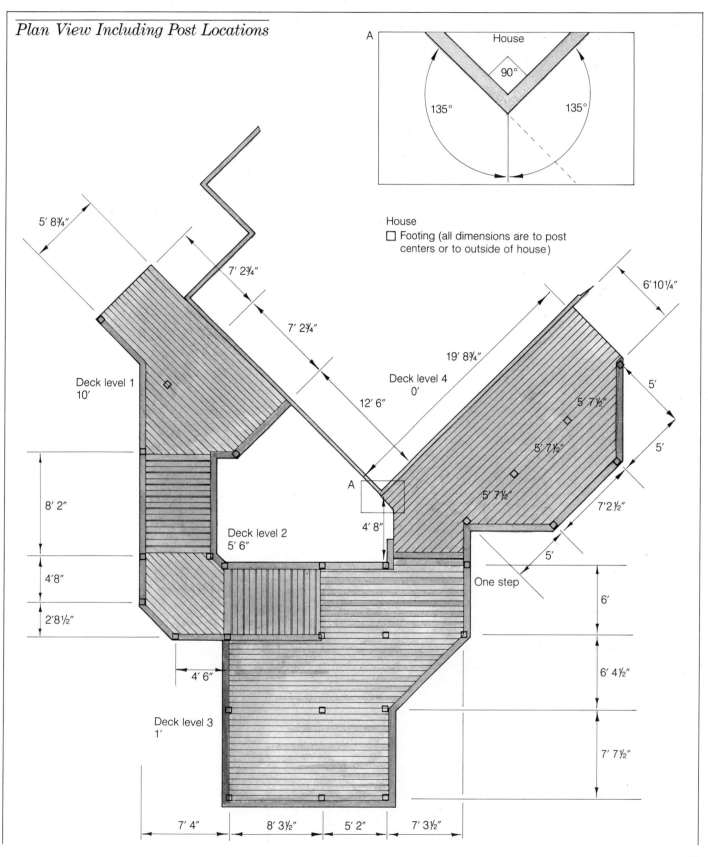

Plan View Including Post Locations

A — House — 90° — 135° — 135°

House
☐ Footing (all dimensions are to post centers or to outside of house)

5′ 8¾″

7′ 2¾″

7′ 2¾″

6′10¼″

19′ 8¾″

Deck level 1
10′

Deck level 4
0′

5′ 7½″

5′

12′ 6″

5′ 7½″

5′

8′ 2″

5′ 7½″

A

5′ 7½″

7′2½″

Deck level 2
5′ 6″

4′ 8″

4′8″

One step

5′

2′8½″

6′

4′ 6″

6′ 4½″

Deck level 3
1′

7′ 7½″

7′ 4″   8′ 3½″   5′ 2″   7′ 3½″

PLAN 11

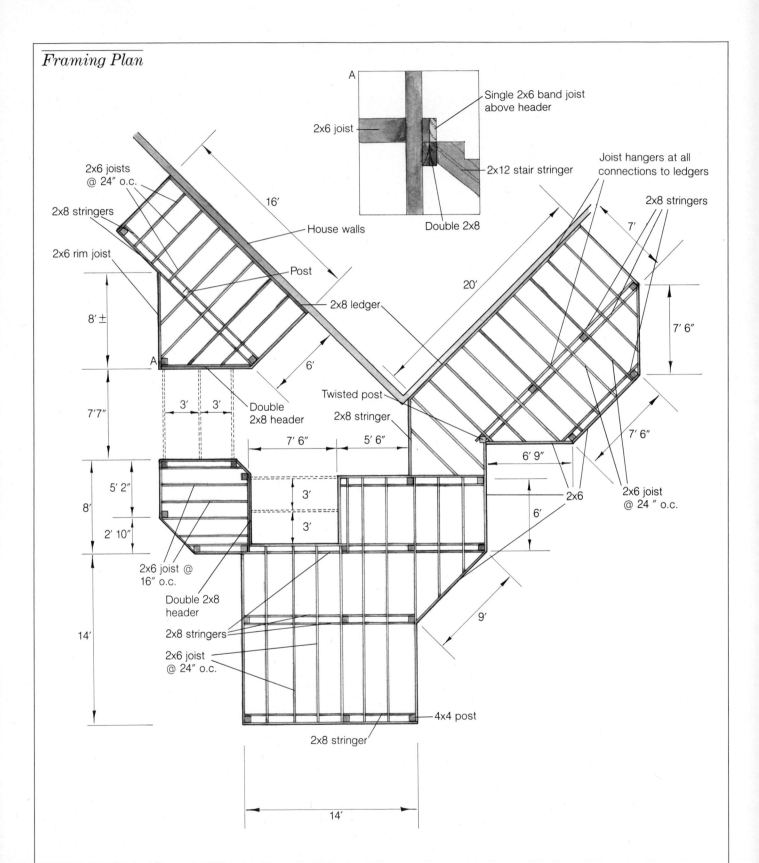

Framing Plan

A

2x6 joist

Single 2x6 band joist above header

2x12 stair stringer

Double 2x8

Joist hangers at all connections to ledgers

2x8 stringers

2x6 joists @ 24" o.c.

2x8 stringers

16'

2x6 rim joist

House walls

Post

2x8 ledger

20'

7'

8' ±

7' 6"

A

6'

Twisted post

Double 2x8 header

2x8 stringer

7' 6"

7'7"

3'   3'

7' 6"   5' 6"

6' 9"

2x6 joist @ 24" o.c.

5' 2"

3'

2x6

6'

8'

2' 10"

3'

2x6 joist @ 16" o.c.

Double 2x8 header

9'

14'

2x8 stringers

2x6 joist @ 24" o.c.

4x4 post

2x8 stringer

14'

The total height separation between the highest and lowest platforms depends on the distance between floor levels in the house—exactly 10 feet in this plan. This overall distance determines the number and height of stair risers. This plan uses 6-inch risers, so 20 are needed altogether. These numbers will vary with site conditions and how steep you want the stairs to be (within code limitations). The important thing is that all stairs within the deck system have the same riser height.

Construction Techniques

This deck is not easy to build because of all the height variations and angles (45 degrees), especially if the site is sloped steeply. The best approach is to build the platforms connected to the house first. Then complete the deck, adjusting measurements to the completed platforms. Building in stages like this is a good approach if you are working with a tight budget.

Layout and Footings

Use the dimensions on the layout plan for laying out string lines to locate the footings and piers.

Although it is possible to build all the footings at once, you may want to do them in stages as suggested above. If the site is sloped, be sure to hold the tape measure level for all measurements. You will probably need a stepladder so you can hold the downhill end of the tape high enough, and a plumb bob to transfer the measurement to the ground.

There are 28 footings in this plan, most of them on the perimeter of the deck. It is critical to locate these footings precisely, because the posts extend through the deck and serve as railing posts as well as structural posts. The design of the footings themselves will vary with site conditions, such as frost depth, stability of the soil, and steepness of the grade.

Ledgers and Posts

Attach the 2 by 8 ledgers to the house following the procedures outlined on page 44. Note that the ledger for the lower deck has a 2 by 8 stringer connected to it near the corner of the house. Be sure that the ledger is well bolted at that point.

The posts vary in length, depending on site conditions. Do not cut them to exact length until the deck platform has been built.

Stringers and Joists

The 2 by 8 stringers should be bolted to the posts with two ⅜-inch zinc-coated bolts at each post. Their ends should not be trimmed flush with the posts' outside edges, but should extend far enough beyond to support the 2 by 6 band joists.

All joists are 2 by 6, either 24 inches or 16 inches on center. Attach them to the ledger with joist hangers. Their free ends are held in place with a band joist, which is also bolted to the vertical posts. Because this band joist functions like a stringer, the joists should be connected to it with joist hangers for maximum strength.

Where joists intersect band joists at 45-degree angles, you can use 45-degree joist hangers, or face-nail three 16-penny (16d) nails through the band joist into the main joist.

The long joists (over 10 feet) require blocking at their midpoint. The longest joists, which are 20 feet, require blocking at two places. If you are not able to get 20-foot joists, you can use shorter joists and lap them over beams.

Section View

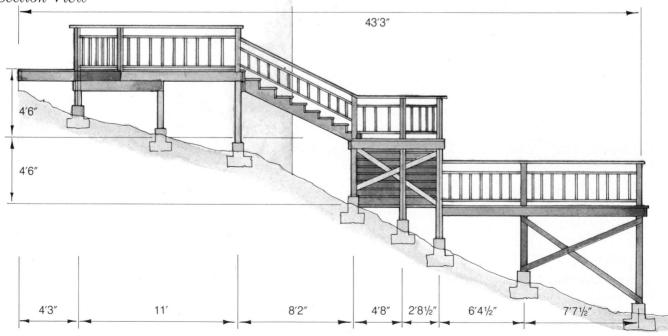

43'3"

4'6"

4'6"

4'3"   11'   8'2"   4'8"   2'8½"   6'4½"   7'7½"

Decking

The 2 by 6 decking is installed perpendicular to the joists, except on the small platform between the two stairways. Here the joists are 16 inches on center, so the decking can be installed diagonally to accentuate the deck's direction of flow.

There is no fascia trim because the deck is intended for a rustic setting and plants will conceal the understructure. Therefore, the ends of the decking boards overhang the band joists 3 or 4 inches. Trim these ends after you install the decking. The overhang should be no more than 1½ inches at the tops of stairs.

Stairs

The two long stairways are supported by three stringers each. Use four stringers if you plan to move heavy loads via the deck. The stringers should be of 3 by 10 or 2 by 12 lumber, and are cut out using standard stair-building techniques (see pages 86-87).

The actual dimensions of each cutout will vary with the overall height separation of the platforms. Be sure to calculate them according to actual heights at the site itself, not the theoretical heights on your plans (they aren't always the same).

Attach the tops of the stringers to the double 2 by 8s with joist hangers. The bottoms rest on the decking boards of the platform below, and should be attached using metal angles or wood cleats.

Before nailing the treads, nail a 2 by 6 riser at each step, making sure its top is flush with the horizontal portion of each stringer's cutout. Then nail or glue the tread stock in place. The number and width of tread pieces depend on your particular stair design. The nosing of each step should overhang the riser below by 1 to 1½ inches.

Railings

The open railing design of this plan uses the 4 by 4 deck posts for the main vertical supports. Measure and cut each post so the top of the cap rail will be 36 inches above the decking (or whatever dimension local codes require).

The horizontal 2 by 4 stringers can be attached to the posts in several manners. The easiest way is to use metal framing clips, shaped like pockets. Attach the clips to the posts first, and then slide the stringers into them. Another way to attach the stringers is with simple toenailing. This works best if you predrill all the holes so the ends of the stringers do not split. A third method is to cut dado grooves in the post and slide the stringers into place. Be sure the wood is seasoned so it won't shrink and leave an ugly gap.

After the stringers are in place, cut and nail each 2 by 2 upright. Their spacing depends on local codes, usually 6 inches or 9 inches maximum. The final step is to attach the 2 by 6 cap rail.

Since the distance between some of the posts is over 6 feet, the railing may tend to sag between them. To prevent this, simply cut a 2 by 4 block that will fit between the decking and the bottom stringer at its midpoint. Do the same between the top stringer and the cap rail.

Materials List

Footings	2.7 cu yd concrete for 28 piers (8"x8"x8") and footings (18"x18"x12")					
	28 metal post anchors					
	56 ⅜"x4½" carriage bolts with nuts and washers					
Framing	Posts	4x4s	4	4' lengths;	6	6' lengths;
			12	8' lengths;	6	10' lengths
			(for steeply sloped site; sites will vary)			
	Ledgers	2x8s	1	16' length;	1	20' length
	Stringers	2x8s	3	8' lengths;	2	10' lengths
			3	12' lengths;	3	14' lengths;
			2	16' lengths;	3	20' lengths
	Band joists	2x6s	3	10' lengths;	4	12' lengths;
			1	14' length;	5	16' lengths
	Joists	2x6s	6	10' lengths;	10	12' lengths;
			3	14' lengths;	4	16' lengths; 3 20' lengths
	Blocking	2x6s	1	12' length;	1	14' length; 1 18' length
	Stair stringers	2x12s	6	10' lengths (or 3x10s: 6 10' lengths)		
	Joist hangers	2x6s	20	2x8s	1	45°
	Ledger bolts	26	⅜"x5" lag bolts and 130 washers			
	Stringer bolts	30	⅜"x5½" with nuts and washers			
		28	⅜"x7" nuts and washers			
		2	⅜"x9" nuts and washers			
		2	⅜"x12" nuts and washers			
Decking and Stair Treads	1685 lineal feet	2x6s	(700 sq ft of deck + 96 sq ft stairs + 2% waste)			
Railings	Stringers	2x4s	12	10' lengths;	6	12' lengths;
			6	14' lengths;	4	16' lengths
	Spindles	2x2s	416 lineal feet (cut into 200 2' pieces + waste)			
	Cap rail	2x6s	1	8' length; 5 10' lengths; 2 12' lengths;		
			4	14' lengths; 2 16' lengths		
Nails	2# joist hanger nails					
	50# 12d HDG common					
	25# 16d HDG common					
	10# 8d finish					

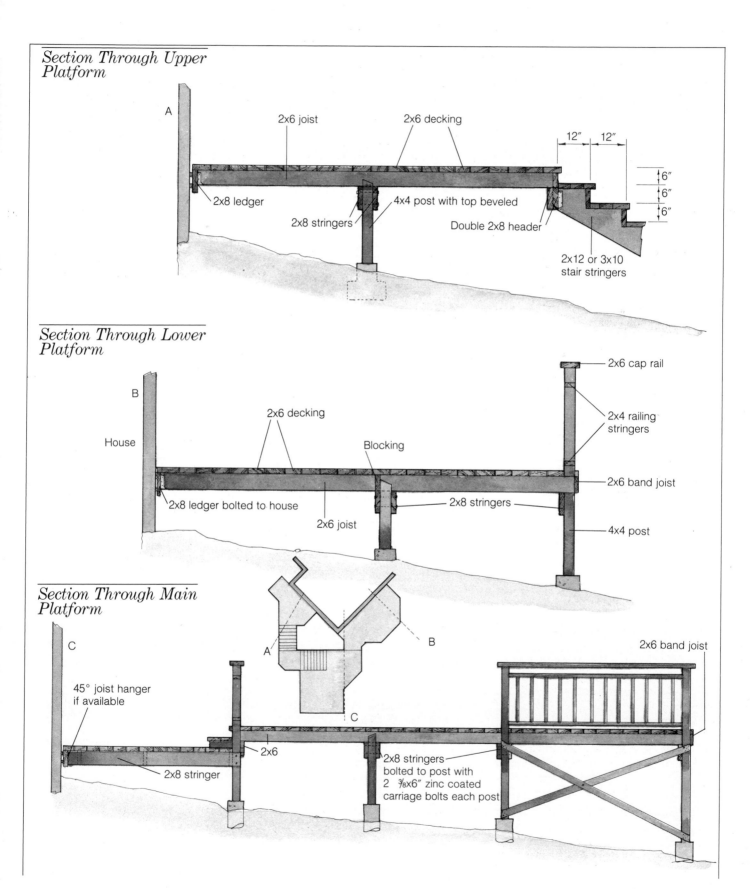

Section Through Upper Platform

A

2x6 joist

2x6 decking

12" 12"

6"
6"
6"

2x8 ledger

2x8 stringers

4x4 post with top beveled

Double 2x8 header

2x12 or 3x10 stair stringers

Section Through Lower Platform

B

House

2x6 decking

Blocking

2x6 cap rail

2x4 railing stringers

2x6 band joist

2x8 ledger bolted to house

2x6 joist

2x8 stringers

4x4 post

Section Through Main Platform

C

A

B

C

45° joist hanger if available

2x6

2x8 stringer

2x8 stringers bolted to post with 2 ³⁄₈x6" zinc coated carriage bolts each post

2x6 band joist

PLAN 12
A Deck and Storage Combination

A deck that is high above ground level offers the benefits of outdoor living space and enclosed space at the same time. If your site requires a tall deck and you wonder what to do with the space beneath it, consider enclosing it. An ordinary deck allows water to drip through and very often creates a chilly, uninviting space below that can affect the mood of the downstairs rooms. This is not a problem if the area is already lost space, such as a steep slope, but if it is part of a well-used yard, you may want to enclose it for storage.

An enclosure solves another common problem of high decks: how to make the understructure more attractive. In this case it is covered with siding to match the house, and the doors and windows enhance it.

Even if you do not need an enclosed space beneath your new deck, you might consider including the roof. It will create a sheltered area

that you could either leave open or enclose and finish at a later time.

The key to this plan is a durable roofing material that is suitable for flat roofs and does not require frequent maintenance or renewal. A variety of such materials allows you to install a permanent wood deck over them. Most of them are rubberlike substances that are painted on. Some are solid membranes that you roll out. Both types are superior to ordinary roll roofing or tar and gravel, but much more expensive. For a recommendation of products that work best in your area, consult a local roofing supplier, sealant specialist, or professional roofing company. You will probably find that some of the materials can withstand direct traffic, but it is advisable to cover them with boards to prolong their life. For all the advantages of this type of roofing, the one main disadvantage is the difficulty of locating leaks. The usual remedy is to recoat the entire surface.

Considerations Before Building

The example featured in this plan includes a deck with covered storage space below. It is shown as an addition to a split-level home and is built over an existing concrete patio. Not all sites will be the same, and there are some particular design issues you must consider before using this plan.

First, what impact will this deck have on downstairs rooms? Will you have to close off windows or add a doorway? Is there a better location for the deck, such as a garage wall?

Second, how will you use the space under the deck? If you are not enclosing it with walls, then you can support the deck with a post-and-beam system. You must plan the number and size of footings, determine whether or not they should be anchored to the house foundation, and seek professional help on techniques.

If you intend to enclose the space for storage or other casual uses, then you can follow this plan. It provides a large door for easy access and two end windows for cross ventilation.

If you wish to use the enclosure for living space, then you must make sure the slab is moisture-proof, add insulation and a heating system, provide access to the house, and include all utility lines, finish work, and fixtures in your plans. Such a project is beyond the scope of this book, but you can consult a professional or refer to such Ortho books as *Basic Carpentry Techniques, Basic Remodeling Techniques,* and *Finish Carpentry Techniques.*

If you are building over an existing concrete patio, make sure that it is structurally sound, that it slopes away from the house at least ¼ inch per foot, and that it is free from subsurface moisture. Such moisture is hard to detect on an open patio, where it can evaporate from the surface, but there is a simple test: tape a piece of plastic to the patio and see if moisture is trapped under it after a day or two.

Structural Features

The framing for this deck is the same as that for any floor system over an equivalent space: 2 by 10 joists, 16 inches on center. In fact, 2 by 8s of structural grades of lumber would be enough for the 12-foot span, but because the framing must carry a roof and possibly a finished ceiling in addition to the deck itself, it is better to use 2 by 10s.

The 12-by-16-foot dimension is convenient for the plywood roof sheathing, but the deck could be built to any size using the same basic structure and joists of the proper size and spacing.

Foundation

An enclosed space requires a continuous perimeter foundation to keep the walls above grade and to provide bearing along the long wall. If the lower floor will be a slab, then the foundation will bear only the deck (one floor). In most areas, codes usually require a 6-inch foundation wall

on a 12-inch-wide footing. If you want the lower floor to be a wood floor on a joist system, then your foundation should be able to support two floors. This usually requires an 8-inch foundation wall on a 15-inch-wide footing.

If the deck is going over an existing concrete slab, you'll need to break through it to excavate for the foundation trenches, unless the slab has a deep footing around its perimeter and your enclosure walls will be located directly over the footing. In this case, you can form and pour a concrete curb directly on top of the footing portion of the slab, or you can attach sill plates to the slab itself if there is a clearance of 6 to 8 inches above the ground. If you need to break through the concrete slab, you can patch it with new concrete after the foundation wall is finished.

For detailed techniques on building a new foundation wall and attaching it to the existing house, see Ortho's books *Basic Remodeling Techniques* and *Basic Carpentry Techniques.*

Plan View of Decking

16'

Railing

12'

Plan View of Room Below

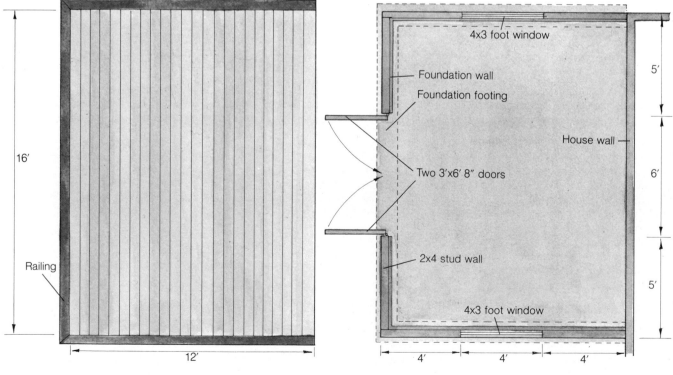

4x3 foot window

Foundation wall

Foundation footing

House wall

Two 3'x6' 8" doors

2x4 stud wall

4x3 foot window

5'

6'

5'

4'   4'   4'

In this example, the existing concrete patio extends beyond the doors of the new enclosure. Therefore, the foundation wall only needs to come up to the level of the slab at the door. All such dimensions will vary with local site conditions and the type of foundation used. See illustration.

Wall Framing
Because the height of the walls depends on the elevation of the deck, you will need to deviate from standard wall framing techniques in two ways. First, frame the long wall and install the roof and floor joists before framing the two end walls. That way you can take exact measurements between the joists and foundation when building the end walls.

Second, calculate the stud lengths for the long wall. Instead of using standard studs, you will have to cut studs to length. Measure the height between the top of the foundation and the upstairs floor level. Subtract the accumulated dimensions of the double top plate, rim joist, plywood roof sheathing, roofing membrane, sleepers, decking boards, ¼-inch-per-foot slope, and foundation sill. The result is the stud measurement for the long wall (except cripple studs over the door header).

Ledger and Joists
The bolting detail for this ledger is different from other decks because it will be protected from the weather, so there is no need to leave a gap between the ledger and wall. Instead, strip away the siding and bolt the ledger against the wall sheathing or framing. Check local codes to see which method is required.

Because the joists slope away from the house, you need to cut their ends at a slight angle so the cuts will be plumb. Also notch the bottom of each joist slightly where it rests in the joist hanger. The other end will not rest flat on the wall plates, so you must bevel it or place a shim between it and the top of the wall plate.

Attach rim joist and install blocking as shown. The rim joist may have to be beveled on the bottom so its top is flush with the tops of the joists.

Wall and Roof Sheathing
Install the wall sheathing or plywood siding first so the roof sheathing will overlap it. For high walls, use 4 by 9 or 4 by 10 sheets to avoid horizontal joints. If the windows and door frame are metal and have nail-on fins, they should be installed before the plywood if it is the finished siding. Otherwise, install them over the plywood sheathing and cover the fins with the finish siding.

Install the tongue-and-groove roof sheathing perpendicular to the joists, staggering the end joints 4 feet and providing gaps along the ends and sides for expansion. The outside edges should be flush with the siding or with any trim attached along the top edge of the siding. Such trim should be installed before the roof sheathing.

Roofing Membrane
Prepare the plywood roof surface for the particular type of roofing material you plan to use. Usually this means caulking all the seams, priming the plywood with a special paint compatible with the membrane, and nailing edge flashing around the edges.

The roofing material is then applied according to the manufacturer's recommendations and allowed to dry thoroughly. Liquid types are applied in three or four coats, often with a drying time of 24 hours in between.

Sleepers and Decking
After the roofing membrane is dry, install the angle flashing against the house, prying siding boards loose so it can be tucked up under the house siding. Then nail 2 by 4 sleepers above all the joists. To keep water from following the nails down through the roof membrane, caulk the bottom of each sleeper where the nails will penetrate it before setting it in place. Also caulk the nail heads after setting them. You also may want to level the deck by putting shims under the sleepers every 16 inches.

Nail the decking boards into the sleepers with 8d or 10d nails so they do not penetrate through the sleepers into the roofing; otherwise, the roof will leak. The outside edge of the decking should overhang the roof by ¼ to ⅜ inch.

Foundation Options

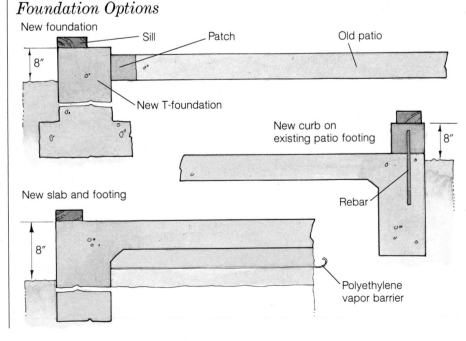

Section View

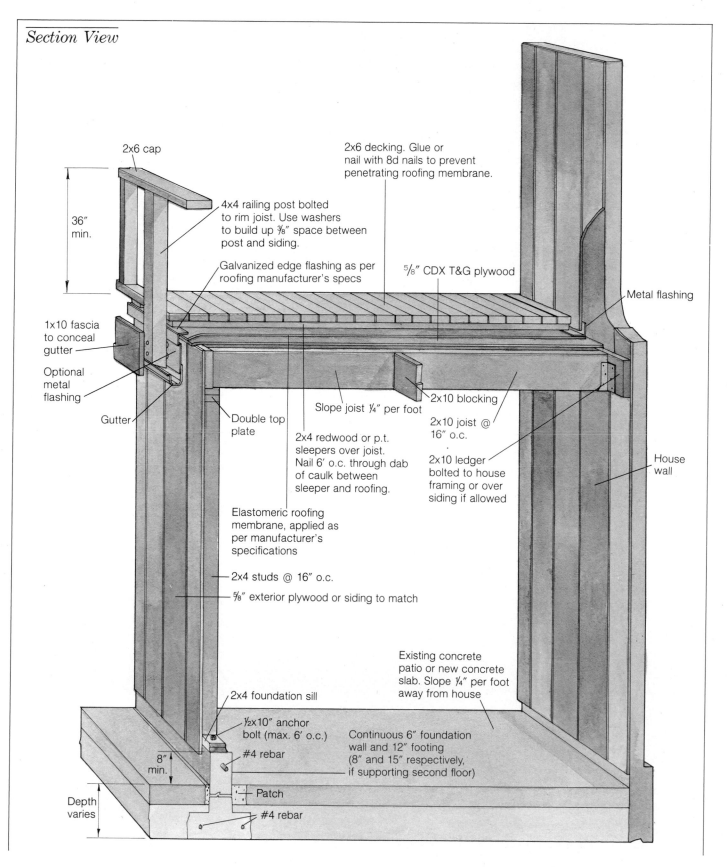

2x6 cap

36" min.

4x4 railing post bolted to rim joist. Use washers to build up ⅜" space between post and siding.

2x6 decking. Glue or nail with 8d nails to prevent penetrating roofing membrane.

Galvanized edge flashing as per roofing manufacturer's specs

⅝" CDX T&G plywood

Metal flashing

1x10 fascia to conceal gutter

Optional metal flashing

Gutter

Double top plate

2x4 redwood or p.t. sleepers over joist. Nail 6' o.c. through dab of caulk between sleeper and roofing.

Slope joist ¼" per foot

2x10 blocking

2x10 joist @ 16" o.c.

2x10 ledger bolted to house framing or over siding if allowed

House wall

Elastomeric roofing membrane, applied as per manufacturer's specifications

2x4 studs @ 16" o.c.

⅝" exterior plywood or siding to match

Existing concrete patio or new concrete slab. Slope ¼" per foot away from house

2x4 foundation sill

½x10" anchor bolt (max. 6' o.c.)

#4 rebar

Continuous 6" foundation wall and 12" footing (8" and 15" respectively, if supporting second floor)

8" min.

Depth varies

Patch

#4 rebar

Railing

The railing shown in this plan is an open style to preserve views as much as possible, but a solid railing could be built using the same posts (see Plans 8 and 9). Bolt them to the siding or trim, if any, so the bolts go through the rim joist. Since this connection is a vulnerable spot for leakage into the wall and possible rot, take precautions by placing washers between the post and siding to create a gap, and by caulking around the bolt holes.

After the posts are installed, nail the top and bottom 2 by 4s to their inside faces. Then nail 2 by 2 spindles to the 2 by 4s, spacing them so the openings do not exceed local code requirements for screening (codes vary from 6 to 9 inches, typically). Then nail on a 2 by 6 cap rail, mitering the corners.

Gutter and Downspout

Install a gutter just below the posts along the long edge of the deck. It should be mounted flush against the siding or fascia board. To prevent water slipping behind the gutter, either caulk it heavily or slide long, straight flashing up under the edge of the roof flashing and slip the back edge of the gutter up under the straight flashing. The flashing will have to be cut to fit around the railing bolts and washers.

If you want to conceal the gutter, nail a 1 by 10 fascia board on the outside of the railing posts so that it drops below the railing posts to cover the gutter. Attach a downspout to one of the ends of the gutter and mount it to the siding.

Finishing the Enclosed Space

Install the doors using jambs, threshold, and casings to match the existing house. Also trim the windows, corners, and any other features of the enclosure to match.

The inside of the enclosure can be left unfinished or can be finished according to its use. If you install plumbing, run a pipe up to the deck so you can add a hose bib.

Materials List

Foundation						
	(40 feet of perimeter foundation; assumes existing slab for floor)					
	1.5 cu yd concrete (for 6"x14" wall and 6"x12" footing)					
	140 feet of #4 rebar (includes 20' for laps + 6 30" dowels into house fdn.)					
	1 roll tie wire					
	10 ½"x10" anchor bolts with nuts and washers					
	Lumber for forms (or use 2x10 joists)					
	Concrete patching materials, as needed					
Shed Framing	Sill	2x4s	1	10' length;	2	12' lengths
	Studs	2x4s	46	8' lengths (or 10' lengths, depending on height of wall)		
	Plates	2x4s	4	12' lengths;	2	16' lengths
	Headers	4x6s (or 2x6s:	1 2	8' length; 8' lengths;	1 1 2	10' length; 10' lengths)
	Ledger	2x10s	1	16' length		
	Joists	2x10s	13	12' lengths;	2	16' lengths (includes blkg.)
	Joist hangers	2x10s	13			
	Shims	1 bdl.				
Sheathing/ Siding	Roof	4x8s	6	⅝" T&G CDX plywood		
	Walls	4x9s	9	⅝" (⅜" min) ext. plywood (or 4x10, if needed)		
Exterior Finish	Roofing	40' galvanized edge flashing				
		16' 3"x3" galv. angle flashing				
		192 sq ft roofing material				
	Windows	2 4'0"x3'0" prehung units to match existing house				
	Doors	2 3'0"x6'8" ext. doors + jambs and hardware				
	Trim	90 lineal feet, for corners, windows, and door (to match existing house)				
Deck	Sleepers	2x4s	13	12' lengths		
	Decking	2x6s	24	16' lengths		
	Railing	4x4s	7	8' lengths		
		2x4s	4	12' lengths;	2	16' lengths
		2x2s	10	10' lengths (cut to 30" each)		
		2x6s	2	12' lengths,	1	16' length
	Bolts	26 ⅜"x6" carriage bolts with nuts and 130 washers (spacers)				
	Fascia	1x10	1	16' length (+ 2 12' lengths, optional)		
	Gutter	16' gutter + hangers and downspout				
Nails and Caulking		2# joist hanger nails				
		12# 8d HDG common or box				
		10# 12d HDG common				
		10# 16d HDG common				
		6 tubes sealant for roof sheathing seams, trim pieces, windows, sleepers				

Deck, Roof, and Framing Plan

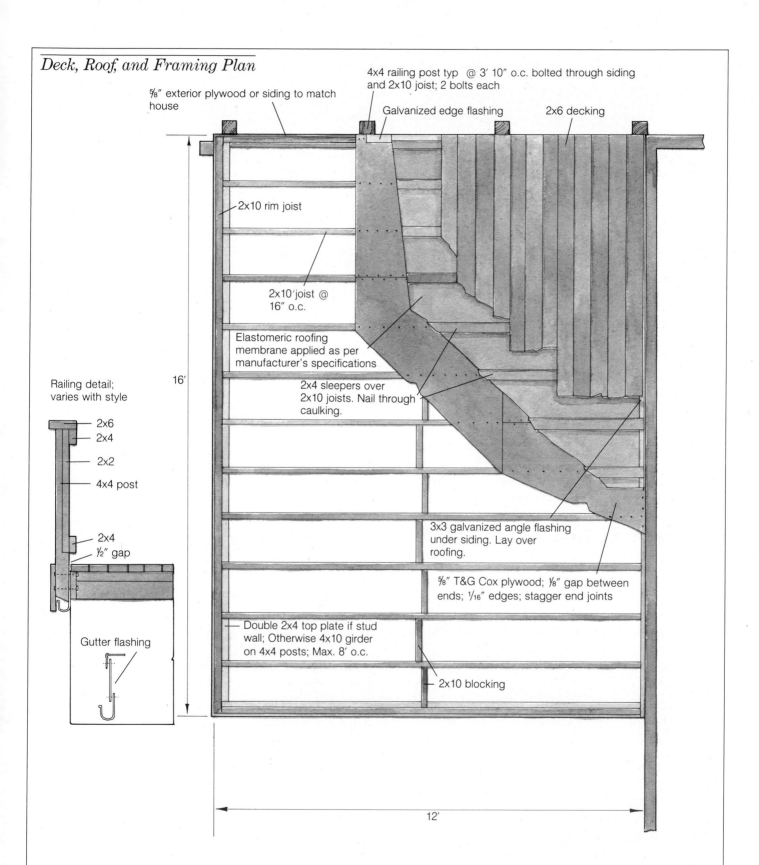

⅝" exterior plywood or siding to match house

4x4 railing post typ @ 3' 10" o.c. bolted through siding and 2x10 joist; 2 bolts each

Galvanized edge flashing

2x6 decking

2x10 rim joist

2x10 joist @ 16" o.c.

Elastomeric roofing membrane applied as per manufacturer's specifications

2x4 sleepers over 2x10 joists. Nail through caulking.

3x3 galvanized angle flashing under siding. Lay over roofing.

⅝" T&G Cox plywood; ⅛" gap between ends; ¹/₁₆" edges; stagger end joints

Double 2x4 top plate if stud wall; Otherwise 4x10 girder on 4x4 posts; Max. 8' o.c.

2x10 blocking

16'

12'

Railing detail; varies with style

2x6
2x4
2x2
4x4 post
2x4
½" gap

Gutter flashing

DECK DETAILS

The trim details of a deck are its surface boards, railings, benches, stairs, and finishes. They can contribute more to a deck's character and appeal than its overall size, shape, or structure can. Together, they transform a deck from an outdoor activity platform to a strong design element in its setting.

This chapter gives you construction details and design criteria to help you choose various finish elements for your deck. By combining them with plans from Chapter 2, you have in this book an almost unlimited choice of deck designs with which to work. It is important that you do not see these details as decorations or afterthoughts to the basic design. You should consider them in the early stages of your planning so they work together with the deck plan to produce a strong, unified structure that fits well into your setting.

This chapter concludes with specific instructions for adapting a deck plan, and a glossary of deck terms. You will find this information useful for working with the plans in Chapter 2 or even for designing your own deck.

There are also tables and charts that will help you size various structural members for a deck. They are typical of those found in most model codes. It is important to emphasize that the size of members called out in these tables is minimum, and for a substantial deck you should always choose the next larger size.

The surface boards, step, and railing are important details of this deck. The decking boards change direction at the step to make it visible and safer, and the change in direction also adds variety and interest to the whole deck. The railing, as a continuous design element, ties all sections of the deck together, and the space below its cap plate helps reinforce that continuity.

The Deck Surface

The deck surface is a strong design element in which small details have a strong impact. Details such as the species and grade of lumber, the board sizes and patterns, nailing patterns, joint patterns, and edging all contribute to the quality of the design. Consider each feature carefully; any one of them could dominate the entire look of the finished deck.

Choosing the Lumber Species and Grade

Five factors will influence your choice of decking lumber: availability, durability, structural requirements, appearance, and cost. From a design point of view, appearance is the critical factor. (See Ortho's book *How to Design & Build Decks & Patios* for a complete discussion of wood characteristics.) This does not mean that you simply choose the most beautiful lumber to have the most beautiful deck. For one thing, there can be wide variation within a given species, and even within the same grade. Also, a poor choice of pattern, sloppy detailing, or weathering can make the most beautiful lumber look shabby; conversely, inferior grades of lumber can be enhanced by staining, careful detailing, and an overall strong deck design. Therefore, it is more important to know what appearance characteristics you are selecting for than to know what are the "best" grades of lumber.

What appearance characteristics should you consider? First, color. If you want the decking to weather, your choice of species is very important. Some woods lighten to a silvery shade of gray (cedar, for instance), and others darken to almost black (redwood). Pressure-treated lumber retains its original color (usually light green or tan), but softens in intensity. If you will stain or paint the deck, your choice of species will depend on its ability to hold stain or paint rather than its color characteristics. For various grades of lumber within a species, the presence of sapwood will affect natural coloring tendencies but not staining or painting qualities.

Decking Patterns

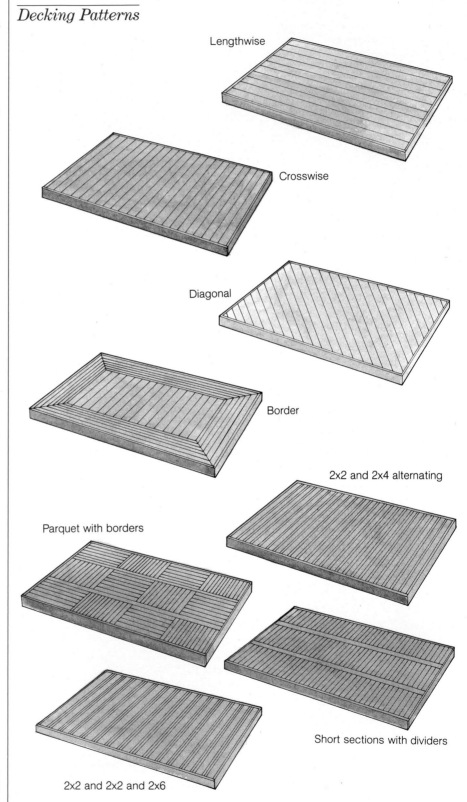

Lengthwise

Crosswise

Diagonal

Border

2x2 and 2x4 alternating

Parquet with borders

Short sections with dividers

2x2 and 2x2 and 2x6

Another appearance factor is grain pattern, designated as *flat grain* or *vertical grain.* Some species and grades of lumber are more likely to have a straight, parallel grain pattern (vertical grain), and others have a wide, curvy pattern (flat grain). Most decks for informal or rustic settings can use flat-grain lumber, but if your setting is formal or has a strong sense of pattern and delineation, then you should choose vertical grain.

Knots and imperfections are another factor to consider. Knot-free, or *clear,* lumber is more expensive than other grades but would be desirable where richness of texture or a smooth, uninterrupted plane are vital design elements. Small decks, or decks that function as focal points as much as activity areas, fall into this category. Decks with a view, or decks with many activity spaces that will include their own focal points, are not as likely to need clear grades of lumber, as long as the knots are small and tight.

Joint Patterns

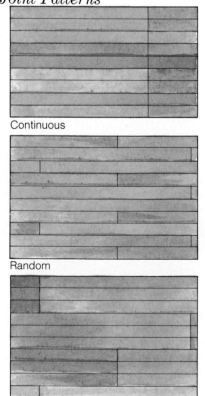

Continuous

Random

Pattern

It is even possible to get mixed orders of lumber with some premium boards and some with imperfections. Use the best boards at doorways, on steps and high-traffic areas, and along the edge of the deck.

Choosing the Size of Lumber

Whether your boards should be 2 by 4s, 2 by 6s, 2 by 2s, or some other size, depends on the pattern you select (see below), but two other considerations will also affect your choice. One is span. Be sure the boards can safely span the distance between joists, especially in diagonal patterns. Also, it is best to avoid boards wider than 2 by 6 because they warp so easily and drain poorly.

Selecting a Pattern

The possibilities for creating patterns out of decking boards are almost endless, but there are only a few that would be successful on any given deck. These general principles, along with the illustrated examples, will help guide you in choosing a pattern.

• On long rectangular decks, boards laid crosswise create a somewhat serene and restful feeling. Boards laid the long way accentuate the length of the deck and ''drive'' you from one end to the next rather than invite you to stay and rest.

• Borders, whether a single trim board or a wide margin, give a finished feeling to the deck.

• On small decks, simple patterns work better than intricate patterns.

• If boards are laid diagonally, it should be for a clear reason. They should reflect a dominant angle in the house or landscape, direct the eye to a clear focal point, or guide traffic to a doorway or stairs.

• Complex or intricate patterns accentuate rather than hide the defects in boards. It would be better to spend money on a premium grade of lumber rather than the labor and wasted material required for complex patterns. Otherwise, simply consider painting the boards.

Choosing a Fastening Option

With the advent of exterior deck adhesives there is now a choice in fastening methods for decking boards. Adhesives have the advantage of a clean, nail-free look, a safe surface with no popped nail heads, and faster installation. Adhesive is more expensive than nails, if you're doing the project yourself, and it is impossible to remove a deck board cleanly once it's in place.

Nails are less expensive than adhesives, but you must be careful to maintain straight lines, choose only high-quality corrosion-resistant nails, and take precautions to avoid splitting the board ends. Nails are better if the decking boards are crooked and need to be straightened as they are installed. They also puncture the top edge of the joists, which over time can lead to water penetration and splitting if the joists are not treated or painted first.

Locating End Joints

If the deck is longer than individual decking boards, the boards will have to be joined at several places. The illustration shows three options: one long, continuous joint; random joints; and an intentional joint pattern. The main thing is to select your option beforehand and follow it consistently.

If the decking is narrow, such as 2 by 3s or 2 by 4s, you should cluster the joints into an intentional pattern so the deck will not look too ''busy'' with joints. With larger sizes of deck boards you can use any of the three options, although a long, continuous joint must be used carefully to avoid dominating the entire deck.

Choosing an Edge Detail

Most plans in this book include a fascia board to trim the edge of the decking. In some cases it is a wide board that covers the joist as well as the decking edge, and in other cases it is a 2 by 4 that creates an additional shadow line around the deck. Of course, leaving the edge of the decking boards exposed is always an option, particularly if plants conceal it.

Railings

Not all decks need railings, but if they do, the railing should be planned at the same time as the rest of the deck. For one thing, its design could influence the deck's basic structure, such as location of posts or size of rim joists. The railing will also have a strong impact on the deck's appearance, and the two should be planned together to ensure harmony and unity of design.

Code requirements will dictate some of the railing's features, such as height (usually 36 inches), maximum distance between railing members (codes vary from 6 to 9 inches), and lateral strength (15 pounds per lineal foot resistance). The rest of the design is up to you, and your choices are almost endless.

Your first consideration should be the aesthetic character of the house and landscape. Is it formal? Does it accentuate horizontal or vertical lines? Are angles prominent? Is there an abundance of delicate and rich detailing? Such questions will help you determine which railing designs may fit better than others. If you are not sure, stay with simple and basic designs.

At the same time that you consider aesthetics, you should also be aware of the railing's functional requirements. Must views be preserved? Is wind a factor? Will you want to set food and drinks on top of the railing? Is privacy needed? Will low flower pots or small objects be placed next to the railing, objects that could slide under a railing that is too high off the deck?

By the time you have answered these questions, the railing will almost have designed itself. Your final task is to evaluate pictures and actual railings for ideas that could satisfy your design criteria.

These four pages are intended to show the construction details for a variety of simple railing designs. They can be adapted to any post arrangement. The method for fastening members together is not specified, since many options are possible. In most cases, metal framing connectors or toenailing using predrilled holes will join boards together when they cannot be face-nailed.

Horizontal Railings

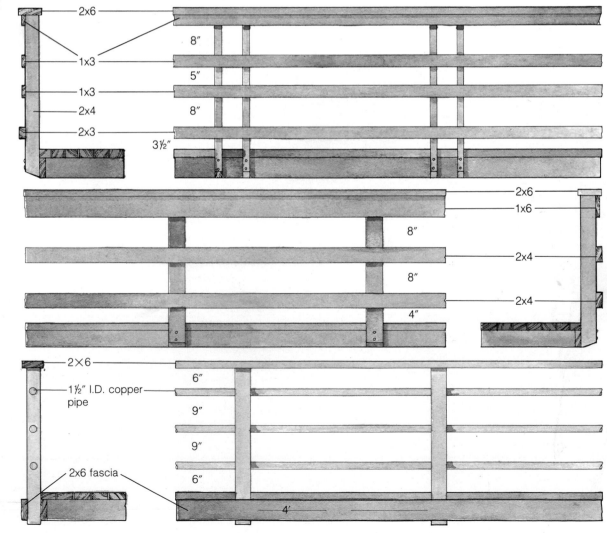

Vertical Railings

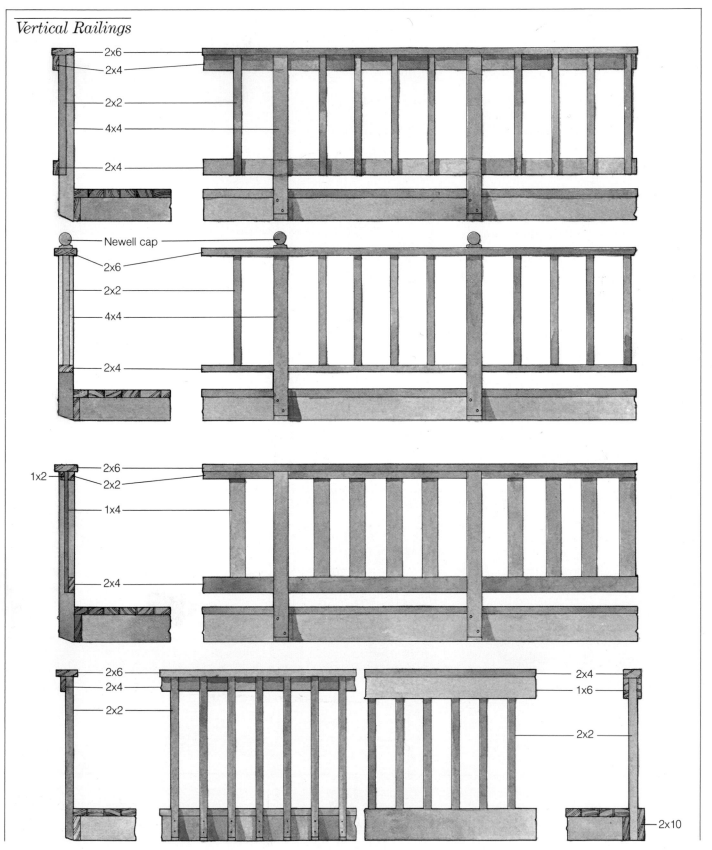

2x6
2x4
2x2
4x4
2x4

Newell cap
2x6
2x2
4x4
2x4

1x2
2x6
2x2
1x4
2x4

2x6
2x4
2x2

2x4
1x6

2x2

2x10

Railings

Railings with a View

There are times when a 36-inch-high railing blocks a desirable view. One solution to this problem is a see-through railing, either of wire mesh or transparent plastic or glass. An attractive wire screening called *welded fabric* comes in rolls of various widths and with various mesh dimensions, such as 1″ x 2″, 2″ x 1″, and 3″ x 3″. It is available galvanized or covered with colored vinyl. Choose a dark color, or spray-paint it so that the wire does not compete with the view behind it. You can attach the wire to the posts and stringers with galvanized poultry wire staples. Hold each staple in place with needle nose pliers to make hammering easier, and align the wire carefully at the very beginning. A crooked start is impossible to straighten later on.

Glass or plastic panels are another see-through option, especially when wind is also a problem. Any glass must meet code requirements, which usually means safety plate or tempered glass. Plastics commonly used are acrylic, which scratches and even splits fairly easily, and polycarbonate, which is very durable but also expensive. Both plastics expand and contract a great deal, so leave room around their edges. They also discolor in time, so check the manufacturer's specifications carefully.

If some privacy is as important as visibility, the answer is a railing that is partially solid but has an opening below the cap rail. The example here uses lattice for the screening, but any solid fencing or siding material could be used.

In addition to the railings described here, some of the railings on pages 80-81 allow you to see distant views. The best patterns are horizontal, especially those using small elements like pipes. They permit eye-level views while you are seated, depending on your distance from the railing and the height of the horizon or other dominant view features.

Solid Railings

Solid railings are featured in several plans in this book. They provide an excellent way to tie a new deck to the existing architecture, since they can be covered with the same siding material as the house. They also give the deck a very finished effect.

The main problems with solid railings are expense and potential moisture damage. They are expensive because finish materials must be installed on both sides of the railing. They are prone to moisture damage because they create covered spaces where water can accumulate. The best way to prevent this problem is to provide a moisture barrier at the top of the railing and to use pressure-treated lumber for framing.

The moisture barrier should be at the top of the railing, under the cap rail, so water won't get inside the railing. You can use heavy building paper, like #30 felt, or have sheet metal caps made up. As long as the siding material is applied carefully, it should waterproof the sides.

The deck side of the railing should have space above the decking boards for water to escape and air to circulate. The outside, however, can either terminate at the same level or extend down beyond the deck surface to become a screen.

Privacy Screens

It may be necessary to provide a tall screen along one or several sides of the deck to retain privacy. Many materials could be used, including siding to match the house, fencing, plants, and fabric. This example shows plywood siding nailed to a simple stud wall that extends below the deck on the outside.

Fencing materials make excellent screens. Use tall posts as the main support members, bolting them to the sides of the deck in the same way as railing posts. Then attach 2 by 4 stringers between them, top and bottom, and install fencing material.

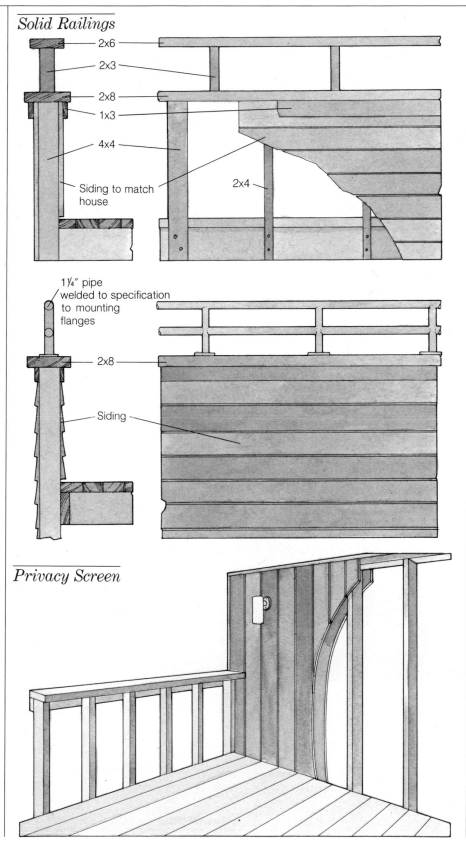

Solid Railings

2x6
2x3
2x8
1x3
4x4
Siding to match house
2x4

1¼" pipe welded to specification to mounting flanges
2x8
Siding

Privacy Screen

Benches

Like railings, benches should be planned along with the deck structure to ensure continuity of design and construction. However, it is also possible to build these benches as freestanding units.

Benches should be from 15 to 18 inches high for comfortable seating, and at least 15 inches deep where they double as a safety railing for low decks. This page shows several designs that use standard lumber in different combinations to produce these dimensions.

The Bench Surface

The bench surfaces feature 2-inch lumber of various widths, all edged by a 1-inch or 2-inch fascia. The corners of the fascia should be mitered to create a very elegant border, which can be further refined by smoothing all the edges with a plane, rasp, or router. There are two methods for assembling the platforms so no nail heads show on the top surface. One is to toenail each slat from the side rather than face-nail it down through the top. This works only for the 2 by 2s or 2 by 4s on edge. The other method is to construct the bench platform upside down, nailing the cleats to the slats from below. Be sure to place the best sides of the boards down when nailing this way.

Bench Construction

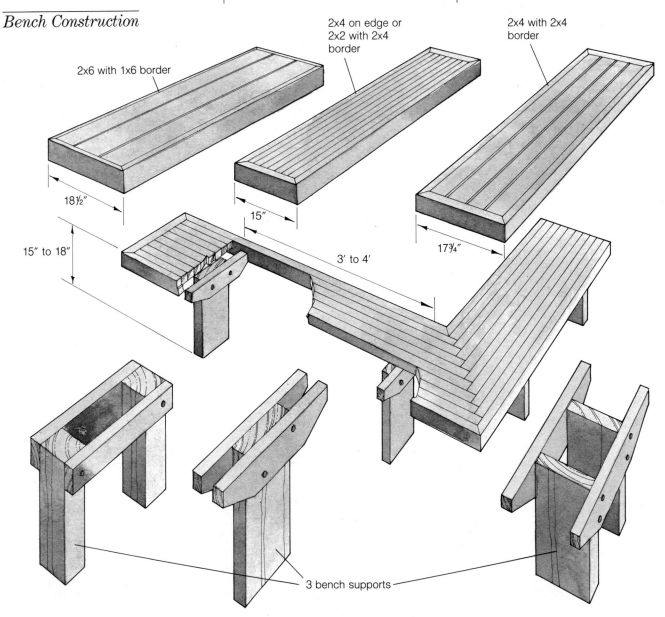

2x6 with 1x6 border

2x4 on edge or 2x2 with 2x4 border

2x4 with 2x4 border

18½"

15"

17¾"

15" to 18"

3' to 4'

3 bench supports

The cleats and uprights can be 2-inch lumber, 4 by 4s, or various combinations. The cleats are beveled at the ends so they do not protrude below the fascia, but in some cases extra-wide cleats could be used so they will show below the platform as an intentional design element.

Attaching the Bench

A freestanding bench can be attached to the deck by toenailing its supports into the deck boards. The supports should be predrilled, to avoid splitting, or secured to the decking with metal brackets. There are several ways to attach the bench's uprights to the deck framing as a permanent part of the structure. One is to extend the deck's supporting posts through the decking boards.

A second way is to bolt uprights to the rim joists or to the field joists during construction. A third way is to attach the bench to the railing posts. This method is particularly appropriate for high decks where a 36-inch railing provides a back for the bench and also meets code requirements. In addition, a rail would have to be installed under the bench to reduce the size of the opening to the minimum 6 or 9 inches.

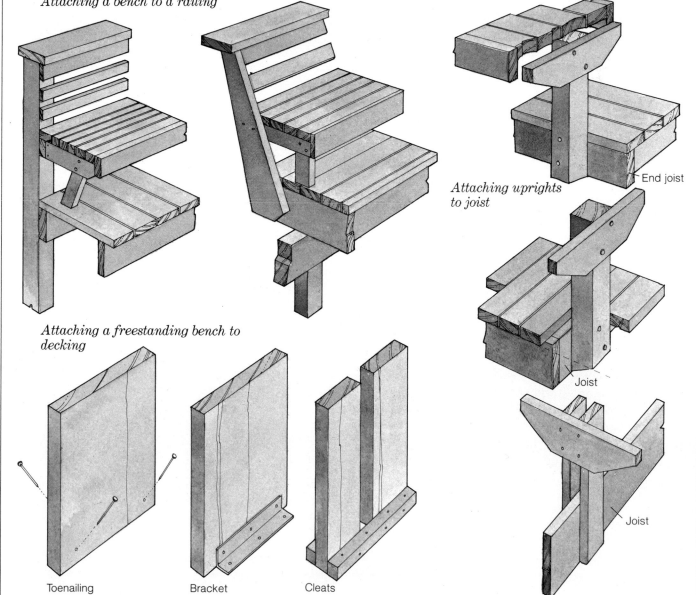

Attaching a bench to a railing

Attaching uprights to joist

End joist

Joist

Joist

Attaching a freestanding bench to decking

Toenailing

Bracket

Cleats

Stairs and Steps

There are many locations where stairs and steps may be needed around a deck: access from the house, access to the garden, changes in platform levels, and connections between separate decks. They may range from a single step to a complete staircase, but it is very important, for safety's sake, that all steps around the same deck level have a constant riser-to-tread ratio.

If one or two steps are needed, the easiest way to build them is to construct small platforms using 2 by 6 or 2 by 8 joists. These dimensions are convenient because the lumber is actually 5½ inches and 7½ inches deep, respectively, which are commonly used riser heights. For steps to the ground, you can use a flat rock or pour a simple concrete step, or improvise wood hanging steps similar to the one shown here.

If a staircase has more than two treads, it should be constructed using stringers (also called carriages). See Ortho's books *How to Design & Build Decks & Patios* and *Basic Carpentry Techniques* for detailed stair-building instructions.

These drawings illustrate some variations for outdoor stairs. The treads themselves should be similar to the decking material, free of knots, and either sloped for drainage or built with more than one board so cracks can be left between them. Consult the table for specific riser and tread dimensions. Note that dimensions refer to the stringer cutouts. The actual tread width will be increased by the amount of overhang, usually 1 to 1½ inches.

The stringers should terminate at a concrete or masonry landing or suitable footing. If the stringers themselves are not made of decay-resistant lumber, they should not be placed directly on the concrete but on 2 by 4 blocks. You can attach the tops of the stringers to the deck using joist hangers, a ledger board, or bolts if there are handy joist or beam ends.

If an open staircase reveals the deck's understructure, you may want

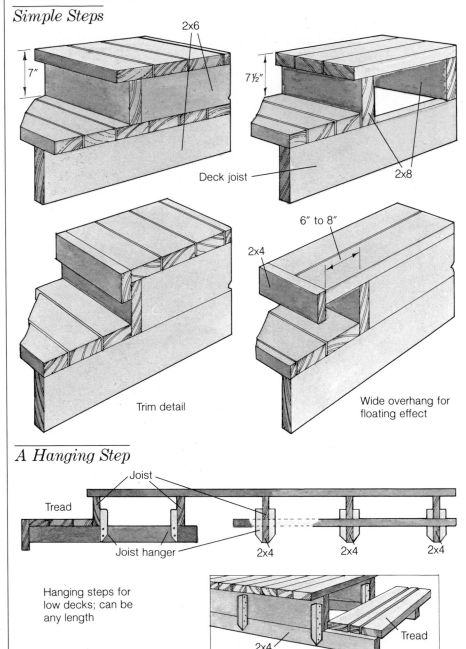

Simple Steps

7"

2x6

7½"

Deck joist

2x8

Trim detail

6" to 8"

2x4

Wide overhang for floating effect

A Hanging Step

Joist

Tread

Joist hanger

2x4   2x4   2x4

Hanging steps for low decks; can be any length

2x4

Tread

to add solid risers for a more finished look. You can use 1 by 6 or 1 by 8 lumber or, for a more refined look, install short pieces of tongue-and-groove siding vertically.

The solid stringer gives stairs a more massive look and accentuates their flow. It is excellent for long stairs where strength is needed. The treads can be attached using wooden cleats or metal stair angles.

Because of their exposure and high concentration of joints, stairs are vulnerable to decay. You should use decay-resistant lumber, treat all cut ends, and leave gaps between boards for air circulation.

Attach railings to stairs with more than three treads or that rise more than 30 inches above grade.

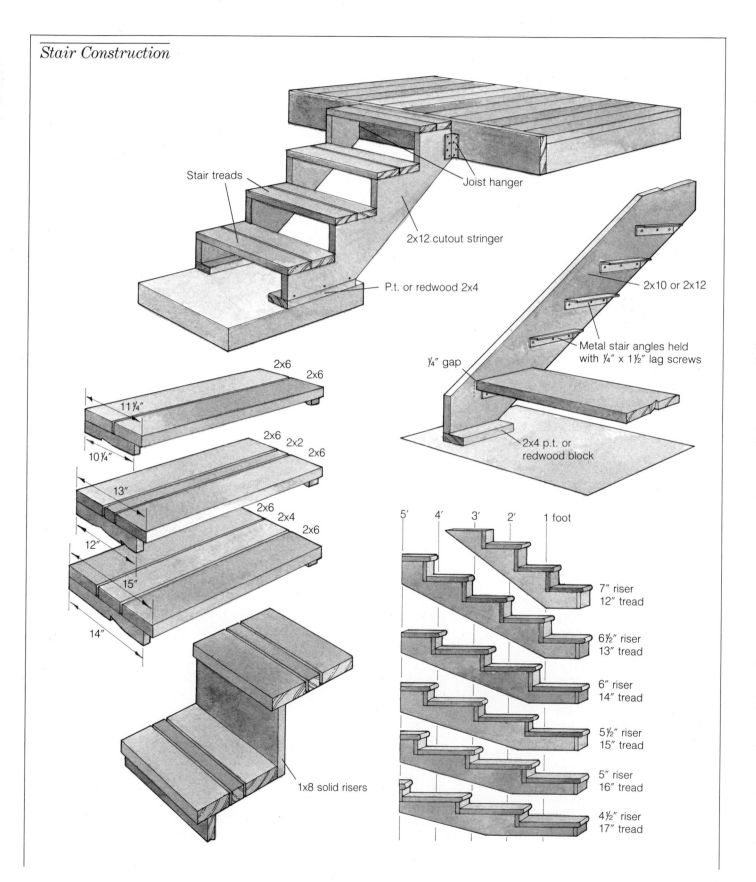

Stair treads

Joist hanger

2x12 cutout stringer

P.t. or redwood 2x4

2x10 or 2x12

1/4" gap

Metal stair angles held with 1/4" x 1 1/2" lag screws

2x4 p.t. or redwood block

2x6

2x6

11 1/4"

10 1/4"

2x6 2x2

2x6

13"

2x6 2x4

2x6

12"

15"

14"

1x8 solid risers

5' 4' 3' 2' 1 foot

7" riser
12" tread

6 1/2" riser
13" tread

6" riser
14" tread

5 1/2" riser
15" tread

5" riser
16" tread

4 1/2" riser
17" tread

Deck Finishes

When you finish building a deck there is a great feeling of accomplishment and satisfaction. You immediately want to put away the tools, set out the furniture, invite some friends over, and have a celebration. However, there is one important step that you should plan on from the moment you begin construction. Your deck is not finished until it's finished. You have to apply some kind of finish to it or take other steps to preserve it.

Deck finishes, such as stains, sealers, paints, and bleaches, are coatings used to increase the wood's durability or to enhance the deck's final appearance. Some do both. There are many ways you can finish your deck, depending on the type of lumber used, your preference of color, and the deck's environment. The following guidelines will give you techniques for selecting a finish and applying it to various kinds of lumber. You may use the same finish throughout the deck, or you may choose to finish different parts in different ways. For example, you could paint the understructure and railings, but stain the decking boards or leave them natural. Or you could stain the decking boards one color and the railings another. The techniques described on these two pages will apply to all parts of the deck.

It is important to realize that both your choice of finish and your choice of lumber play major roles in the deck's final look and its ability to withstand constant exposure to the elements, so consider these factors early in your planning.

An issue related closely to finishes is the health risk of handling certain toxic wood preservatives. The Environmental Protection Agency has banned a number of preservatives from over-the-counter sales and restricted their use to licensed applicators and manufacturers of pressure-treated lumber. The restricted list includes creosote, pentachlorophenols, and inorganic arsenic compounds. Others may be added.

Since the restricted preservatives will not even be available for use by homeowners, you do not have to worry about the health risks of handling them. However, the risks vary with respect to lumber that is already treated. You should use any lumber that has been treated with pentachlorophenol for structural members only, or cover it with two coats of a nonpreservative sealer. Avoid creosote-treated lumber altogether. Lumber treated with inorganic arsenic compounds (such as chromated copper arsenate) can be used for deck boards and railings. Preservative-treated lumber should not be used, however, for any food surfaces or surfaces that expose skin to prolonged contact. All restrictions and recommendations regarding wood preservatives may change, so check with a competent retailer or local environmental authorities before making a final decision.

When you work with pressure-treated lumber, take safety precautions in cutting it. Wear goggles and a respirator, and gloves if the wood is damp. When you finish the job, do not dispose of scraps by burning. Take them to a dumping site approved for preservative disposal.

Finish Options: The Natural Look

Weathered wood. If you want your deck to have a gray, weathered look, the easiest "finish" is to do nothing. Just let it weather naturally. This technique works best with all-heart grades of a durable species (cedar, cypress, redwood), although pressure-treated lumber also weathers well even if the color is not strictly the same as the natural wood.

The final color and the length of the aging process vary with the type of lumber and its exposure on the deck, but generally cedar and cypress weather to a light, silvery gray, redwood turns dark gray, and pressure-treated lumber turns into a lighter tint of its original green or tan.

It takes from one to two years for complete weathering, and the colors go through various intermediate stages. For this reason, there may be times during the aging process when the deck looks out of place.

To accelerate the weathering process and give more uniform results, you can apply a wood bleach. It works best on wood with no preservative or water repellant. (If the wood has been treated, wait at least 60 days before applying the bleach.) To apply bleach, brush or roll it onto the deck, wait the specified period of time, and then hose it off, as per the manufacturer's instructions. Renew the bleach treatment periodically if the deck darkens. The bleach has no preservative value, although you should make sure to buy a brand that includes a mildewcide.

If your wood is neither pressure-treated nor a durable species, and you still want a weathered look, you should apply a clear sealer or water repellant. Sealers can also be used on durable species of lumber to prolong their life and enhance their richness. Choose a type that penetrates rather than forms a hard shell on the surface of the wood, since the shell will quickly crack as the wood expands and contracts. A clear sealer will delay the weathering process a few months, but will not retard it altogether. For quicker weathering, you could bleach the wood first and then apply the sealer. Renew the sealer every two or three years, as needed.

New wood. A just-built deck of fresh, new wood has a beauty most people admire. The warm tones of the wood, its grain, its texture, and even its smell create a clean and appealing deck that seems to blend with almost any setting. Inevitably, however, the wood ages and the deck loses that same freshness.

Is there some way to capture that look of new wood permanently? Although there is no way to preserve the exact look, there are three possible treatments that approximate or imitate it.

One option is to prolong the look by applying a clear sealer. This protects the wood and slows down the weathering process by as much as a year, giving you more time to enjoy the wood's original color before having to do something else. Use a water-repellant sealer that penetrates the wood.

The second option is to apply no finishes or sealers at all and let the wood weather naturally. Then restore its surface periodically by scrubbing it with trisodium phosphate (TSP) and applying oxalic acid or a special deck-renewing product available for this purpose. (Be sure to follow the manufacturer's safety precautions, including the use of rubber gloves.) After rinsing off the acid, you will have a deck instantly transformed from gray to original-looking wood. It will not have that smooth, clean surface of brand new wood, but it will have a rich, warm tone instead of weathered gray. Do not use this method unless the wood is resistant to decay, or it will not last long. To maintain the look, you need to repeat this treatment whenever the deck weathers to an objectionable color.

The third possible treatment is to stain the deck a color that matches the new wood as closely as possible. The stain will cover the wood with a colored coating, but the wood's grain and texture will still show clearly as long as you use a semitransparent stain. Wait for the deck to dry out, usually 60 days. If you have applied a sealer to the deck, also wait at least 60 days before staining, or until the deck loses its natural new-wood look. Use a semitransparent, light-bodied stain specified as nonchalking or sealer type. It is best to do small samples first, until you are sure the stain is the color you desire. Some stains include a water-repellant additive, or even an approved preservative. Use this type of stain for wood that has had no other treatment, unless it is a durable species. You can make your own by mixing equal parts of a stain and a sealer or approved preservative.

Finish Options: A Custom Color

If the color of natural wood, either weathered or new, is not suitable for your deck, you can change it to almost any color imaginable by staining or painting it.

Staining. Exterior stains penetrate the wood rather than coat it like paint, leaving the surface texture the same as natural wood, but a different color. Two types of stains are available: semitransparent (light-bodied) and solid (full-bodied). The semitransparent stains have less pigment than solid stains. They reveal the grain of the wood better, but they are not as durable, do not hide wood defects as well, and need to be renewed more often. Both have the advantage of retaining the soft texture and warmth of wood. Stains work particularly well with unsurfaced or resawn lumber.

Most brands offer a fairly wide selection of colors, although the range is limited to earth tones (certain browns, reds, greens, and grays).

It is difficult to predict the exact color of your deck because the same stain will produce a different color on different types of wood, and will even vary between sapwood and heartwood of the same species.

Oil-based stains work better for decks than water-based stains, because they are easier to renew. They work best in combination with a water repellant or approved preservative, either mixed in with the stain or applied 60 days prior to staining. In all cases the deck lumber must be thoroughly seasoned and dry before applying stain. A new deck should stand for two months before staining. If you are staining the deck surface itself, use a light-bodied stain instead of a full-bodied one. The inevitable wear will not be as noticeable, and periodic re-staining will produce a more even color. Just be sure it is a nonchalking or sealer type of stain, so a powdery film does not get tracked into the house.

Painting. Painted decks, or components of a deck, are very effective in achieving an elegant, refined look. Unlike stain, paint completely masks the wood, making it an ideal finish for lower grades of lumber. Paint offers an unlimited choice of colors, and they will not vary with the type of lumber used. Paint takes more time to apply, is more expensive, and is harder to maintain than other finishes, but the extra effort may be worth it. However, once you have painted a deck, it will be impossible to change to any of the other finish options.

For best results, the wood should be thoroughly seasoned before painting, usually 60 days. However, you can prime it beforehand, especially the ends and edges of structural members that get covered up as the deck is built. It is also recommended to apply a water-repellant sealer to the wood before priming, giving it at least two days to dry. The primer itself should be zinc-free, preferably oil-based instead of water-based, and chemically compatible with the final top coat. Use acrylic latex or a high-gloss alkyd paint for the top coats, applying two coats for best results.

If you are painting the deck surface itself, choose a paint specified for outdoor decks or porches so it will withstand heavy wear. Like painted porches and steps, a painted deck surface can be slippery when wet. As an extra safety precaution, especially around doorways and stairs, you can mix a handful or so of clean sand with paint used for the final coat.

Maintaining Your Deck

In addition to applying a finish to your deck, you can prolong its life even more by cleaning and scrubbing it periodically. Use a bleach or other strong cleaner if the boards have any moss or fungus, and remove sand, gravel, and other debris as soon as possible.

APPENDIX
How to Adapt a Plan From This Book

Basic Deck Components

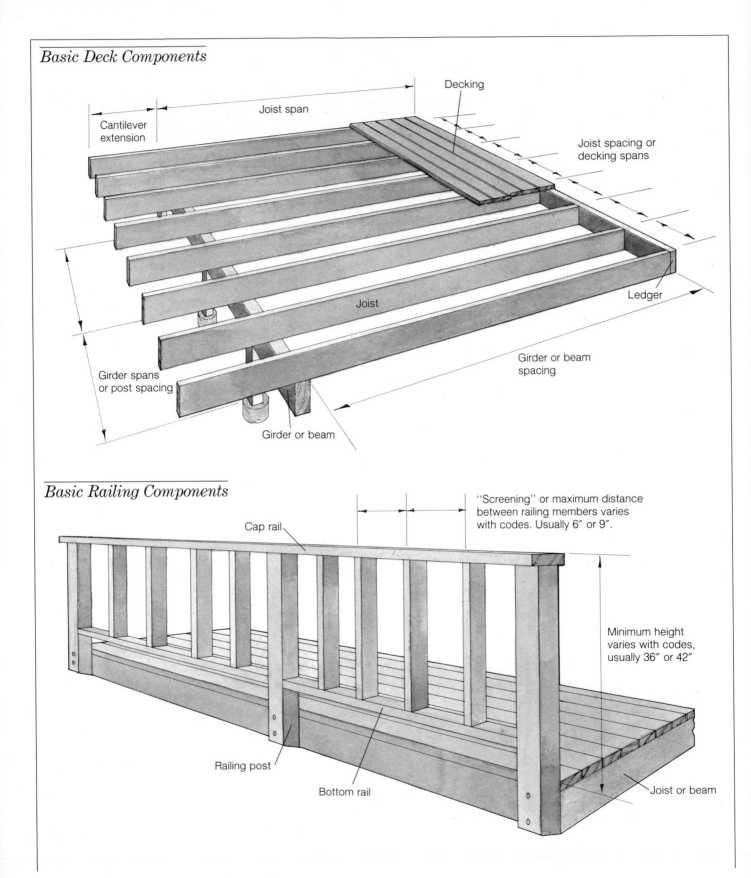

Cantilever extension

Joist span

Decking

Joist spacing or decking spans

Joist

Ledger

Girder spans or post spacing

Girder or beam spacing

Girder or beam

Basic Railing Components

Cap rail

"Screening" or maximum distance between railing members varies with codes. Usually 6" or 9".

Minimum height varies with codes, usually 36" or 42"

Railing post

Bottom rail

Joist or beam

Starting Points

Whether you are looking through this book for ideas and inspiration to design your own deck, or you intend to use one of the plans with little or no alteration, you are more apt to find a deck just right for you if you know exactly what you are looking for. Use the design principles described in Chapter 1 to help you identify your goals and priorities.

After you have picked a plan, you may need to adapt it to fit your particular situation. The following list discusses most of the changes you would want to make. These general principles can be applied to any deck, even though they describe a deck that is attached to a house.

To Enlarge a Deck

If you want to expand the deck outward from the house, the easiest way is to lengthen the joists. You can safely extend them beyond the beam (this extension is called a cantilever) as long as the length of the cantilever section is less than half the joist span between beam and ledger. If you need to extend the deck even farther, you can add a second beam or move the first beam out and make all the joists larger.

To expand the deck along the length of the house, simply lengthen the ledger and beam and add more joists. The longer beam will require an additional footing or two, or you can enlarge the beam and increase the spacings between posts.

In addition to the structural changes, you will also have to increase the number or length of decking boards and make any railings or benches proportionately longer.

To Make a Deck Smaller

To shorten a deck along its length, reduce the number of joists and use shorter decking boards. The beam and ledger must also be shortened accordingly. If you want the deck narrower, move the beam closer to the house and use shorter joists. You will also need fewer decking boards.

To Change a Deck's Shape

The easiest changes involve variations on a basic rectangle. For instance, wrapping a deck around a corner of the house or adding an extension will change the deck from a rectangle to an L. Structurally, this change involves the same principles as enlarging a deck, except that you are lengthening some of the joists instead of all of them, adding a short beam under the new addition instead of under the entire deck, and so on.

Another approach to varying the basic rectangle is to think of an L shape, or a T or a Z, as separate decks joined together. Design the main platform, following the plan you are using, then design the additional leg as a separate deck to be joined to it.

Building angles into an existing plan is also quite simple, if it involves no more than cutting a 90-degree corner so it is two 45-degree angles, or one 30- and one 60-degree angle. To "bend" an entire deck, however, involves redesigning the entire structural system to be sure all the spans and cantilever extensions are within the limitations of the materials.

Recommended maximum spans for spaced deck boards[1]

Species group[2]	Maximum allowable span[3] (inches)					
	Laid flat				Laid on edge	
	1x6	2x3	2x4	2x6	2x3	2x4
1	24	28	32	48	84	96
2	16	24	28	42	72	84
3	16	24	24	36	60	72

[1]These spans are based on the assumption that more than one floorboard carries normal loads. If concentrated loads are a rule, spans should be reduced accordingly.
[2]Group 1—Douglas fir, larch, and southern pine; Group 2—Hem fir and Douglas fir south; Group 3—Western pines and cedars, redwood, and spruces.
[3]Based on Construction grade or better (Select Structural, Appearance, no. 1 or no. 2).

Joist spans (beam spacing)[1]

Species group[2]	Joist size (inches)	Joist spacing		
		16"	24"	32"
1	2x6	9'9"	7'11"	6'2"
	2x8	12'10"	10'6"	8'1"
	2x10	16'5"	13'4"	10'4"
2	2x6	8'7"	7'0"	5'8"
	2x8	11'4"	9'3"	7'6"
	2x10	14'6"	11'10"	9'6"
3	2x6	7'9"	6'2"	5'0"
	2x8	10'2"	8'1"	6'8"
	2x10	13'0"	10'4"	8'6"

[1]Joists are on edge. Spans are center to center distances between beams or supports. (Based on 40 p.s.f. deck live load plus 10 p.s.f. dead load. Grade is no. 2 or better; no. 2 medium-grain southern pine.)
[2]Group 1—Douglas fir, larch, and southern pine; Group 2—Hem fir and Douglas fir south; Group 3—Western pines and cedars, redwood, and spruces.

How to Adapt a Plan From This Book

To Change the Deck's Height

You can raise or lower a deck by changing the heights of its posts. If you are adapting a ground-level deck plan for higher floor levels, be aware of the maximum deck height allowed before a railing is required (usually about 30 inches above the ground). If your proposed height requires posts longer than 5 feet, you should add diagonal cross-bracing.

If you are lowering a deck so it will be closer to the ground, you can change its structure to a beam system with no joists and you can also excavate in order to maintain at least an 8-inch clearance between earth and wood. You should also use heart redwood or pressure-treated material for decks close to the ground.

To Make a Single-Level Deck Multilevel

For a one-step change in level, design the main platform as in the existing plan. If the smaller platform is to be raised, run joists under it just as if the deck were all one level. However, instead of laying decking boards on the joists where the platform is to be raised, run another set of joists crosswise on top of the first ones. Their depth should be the same as the desired height of the step, usually 7½ inches. With this method, the decking on the raised platform will run perpendicular to the main decking, making the change in level more obvious and less hazardous.

If the second level is lower than the main platform or separated by several steps, it is easiest to design it as a separate deck system and join it to the main platform. Footings will usually be in the same places, as if the deck were all one level, but posts under the secondary section of deck will be lower or higher than the main platform. Where the two decks meet, the same posts can support both levels; just attach a stringer to the sides of the posts for the lower deck, and place a beam on top (or bolt another stringer, if the posts are to extend through the deck to become railing supports). See plans 5, 7, 8, 9, and 10 for examples of multilevel decks.

To Change Footings

Some areas may require deeper or larger footings than those used in the plan you have selected. The structure of the deck can remain the same. All you have to do is redesign the footing and pier. For deep footings, usually called for because of frost conditions, an excellent design is a continuous concrete column formed by a fiber tube, with between 1 and 4 vertical reinforcing bars. For steep sites, local codes may require drilled footings, or that all the footings be connected by concrete grade beams.

You may need to change the number or location of footings, to minimize digging, to avoid utility lines, or to take advantage of existing footings from an old deck. Such changes generally require redesigning the structure of the deck to reflect new joist and beam spans.

To Vary the Pattern of Decking Boards

The easiest variation is to use different size decking boards—for instance, 2 by 4s instead of 2 by 6s—or to alternate decking boards of different sizes. If you want to use smaller boards than those in the plan, make sure the boards will safely span the distance between joists.

In some cases you can also change the direction of the decking boards. For example, if the plan shows them running across the joists in perpendicular fashion, you can easily run them diagonally in either direction, as they will still be supported by the joists. Or if the plan shows diagonal decking boards, you can run them perpendicular to the joists or to the original diagonal direction. However, you cannot run the decking boards parallel to the joists without changing the entire structural system.

To Alter Railings

You may need to change the height of a railing to comply with local codes. Simply change the height of each post accordingly, and add or delete intermediate members or alter spacings to make up the difference. Other simple changes include varying the length of the railing or changing the locations of openings. In both cases, add posts where a railing terminates or changes direction. Then move other posts, if necessary, to maintain uniform spacing between all the posts.

Minimum post sizes[1] (wood beam supports)

Species group[2]	Post size (inches)	Load area[3]: beam spacing x post spacing (square feet)									
		36	48	60	72	84	96	108	120	132	144
1	4x4	Up to 12' →→→→→→→→ Up to 10' hts. →→→ Up to 8' hts.									
	4x6					Up to 12' hts. →→→→→→ Up to 10'					
	6x6								Up to 12'		
2	4x4	Up to 12'	Up to 10' hts. →Up to 8' hts. →→→→→→								
	4x6				Up to 12' hts. →Up to 10' hts. →→→						
	6x6						Up to 12' hts. →→→→				
3	4x4	Up to 12'	Up to 10'→Up to 8' hts. →→ Up to 6' hts. →→→→								
	4x6	Up to 12'→Up to 10' hts. →Up to 8' hts. →→→→									
	6x6	Up to 12' hts. →→→→→→→→→→									

[1]Based on 40 p.s.f. deck live load plus 10 p.s.f. dead load. Grade is Standard and Better for 4 by 4 inch posts and No. 1 and Better for larger sizes.
[2]Group 1—Douglas fir, larch, and southern pine; Group 2—Hem fir and Douglas fir south; Group 3—Western pines and cedars, redwood, and spruces.
[3]Example: If the beam supports are spaced 8 feet, 6 inches, on center and the posts are 11 feet, 6 inches, then the load area is 98. Use next larger area 108.

The easiest way to change the style of the railing is to keep the post arrangement called for by the plan and alter the size or configuration of the other railing members, such as cap rail, stringers, and spindles. Because almost all railing systems begin with posts that are spaced 3 to 6 feet apart, you can put these in place and then attach horizontal rails and stringers, which in turn hold up any vertical members between the posts. If you choose a railing design that has a different post arrangement from the one in the plan, you can bolt posts to the band joist or a 2-by fascia board. Lay out the posts so the spacings are equal for each side of the deck.

To Change Steps or Stairs

You'll almost certainly have to adapt any stairs between the deck and the ground to suit your own site. The most important consideration is to make sure that all steps in a flight of stairs are exactly the same height, and that riser and tread dimensions comply with local codes.

Steps between deck levels or between the house and the deck will probably be the same dimensions as those in the plan. However, you can vary the design by using different types of tread lumber, different sizes of boards, or different size overhangs.

You can also add risers or kickboards, if they are not included in the plan, to produce a more finished look.

To Change Planters and Trim Details

There is no limit to the decorative touches you can add to your deck, such as planters and fascia boards, since in most cases they are add-ons that require no structural changes. The only limitations are aesthetic—be sure that these details harmonize with the house and yard, that they are not excessive, that they do not call undue attention to themselves, and that they maintain proportions similar to those of the deck itself.

Beam spans (post spacing)[1]

Species group[2]	Beam size (inches)	Beam spacing[3] (feet) (joist span)								
		4	5	6	7	8	9	10	11	12
1	4x6	Up to 6' →								
	3x8	Up to 8' →		Up to 7'	Up to 6' →					
	4x8	Up to 10'	Up to 9'	Up to 8'	Up to 7' →		Up to 6' →			
	3x10	Up to 11'	Up to 10'	Up to 9'	Up to 8' →		Up to 7' →		Up to 6' →	
	4x10	Up to 12'	Up to 11'	Up to 10'	Up to 9' →		Up to 8' →		Up to 7' →	
	3x12			Up to 12'	Up to 11'	Up to 10'	Up to 9' →	Up to 8' →		
	4x12			Up to 12' →		Up to 11'	Up to 10' →		Up to 9' →	
	6x10						Up to 12'	Up to 11'	Up to 10' →	
2	4x6	Up to 6' →								
	3x8	Up to 7' →		Up to 6' →						
	4x8	Up to 9'	Up to 8'	Up to 7' →		Up to 6'				
	3x10	Up to 10'	Up to 9'	Up to 8'	Up to 7' →		Up to 6' →			
	4x10	Up to 11'	Up to 10'	Up to 9'	Up to 8' →		Up to 7' →			Up to 6'
	3x12	Up to 12'	Up to 11'	Up to 10'	Up to 9'	Up to 8' →		Up to 7' →		
	4x12			Up to 12'	Up to 11'	Up to 10' →		Up to 9' →	Up to 8' →	
	6x10			Up to 12'	Up to 11'	Up to 10' →		Up to 9' →		
3	4x6	Up to 6'								
	3x8	Up to 7'	Up to 6'							
	4x8	Up to 8'	Up to 7'	Up to 6' →						
	3x10	Up to 9'	Up to 8'	Up to 7'	Up to 6' →					
	4x10	Up to 10'	Up to 9'	Up to 8' →		Up to 7' →	Up to 6' →			
	3x12	Up to 11'	Up to 10'	Up to 9'	Up to 8'	Up to 7' →		Up to 6' →		
	4x12	Up to 12'	Up to 11'	Up to 10'	Up to 9' →		Up to 8' →	Up to 7' →		
	6x10			Up to 12'	Up to 11'	Up to 10'	Up to 9' →	Up to 8' →		

[1]Beams are on edge. Spans are center to center distances between posts or supports. (Based on 40 p.s.f. deck live load plus 10 p.s.f. dead load. Grade is no. 2 or better; no. 2, medium-grain southern pine.)
[2]Group 1—Douglas fir, larch and southern pine; Group 2—Hem fir and Douglas fir south; Group 3—Western pines and cedars, redwood, and spruces.
[3]Example: If the beams are 9'8" apart and the species is Group 2, use the 10' column; 3x10 up to 6' spans, 4x10 up to 7', etc.

Deck Terms

Adhesive. Outdoor construction adhesive specified for decks, used instead of nails for attaching decking boards.

Anchor. Metal device embedded in wet concrete for attaching posts to piers.

Baluster. Vertical railing member, held between top and bottom rails.

Band joist. Joist attached to the ends of field joists. Sometimes refers to any joist on the perimeter of the deck. Also called rim joist.

Beam. Major structural member. The thick horizontal timber that rests on top of posts and in turn supports joists or decking. Can be solid or built up of 2 or more 2-bys. Also called a girder.

Blocking. Short pieces of lumber cut from joist material and nailed perpendicularly between joists to stabilize them.

Bracing. Diagonal crosspieces nailed and bolted between tall posts, usually over 5 feet.

Cantilever. The end portion of a joist, or of the entire deck, that extends out beyond the beam.

Cap rail. Topmost horizontal railing member.

Cleat. Short nailer for supporting decking boards or stair treads.

Corrosion-resistant connectors. Fastening hardware—nails, bolts, and sheet metal devices—suitable for outdoor use. Common materials are stainless steel, aluminum, and galvanized (zinc-coated) steel.

Deck boards. Boards used for the actual surface of the deck. Sometimes called decking.

Durable species. Wood species that are naturally resistant to decay and insect damage, such as heart redwood, heart cedar, tidewater cypress, and some locusts. Sometimes refers to other woods that have been pressure-treated.

Earth-wood clearance. The minimum distance required between the ground and any wood. The exception is pressure-treated or durable species lumber specified for ground contact.

Elevation. Drawing of a proposed structure as it looks from the side.

Fascia. Nonstructural, horizontal trim piece that covers the ends of deck boards and part or all of the band joist.

Finish. A coating, such as a stain, paint, or preservative, applied to a deck to color it and protect it against weathering.

Flashing. Aluminum or galvanized sheet metal used to cover joints where moisture might enter a structure.

Footing. The bottom portion of any foundation or pier; it distributes weight to the ground. For decks, it often refers to the concrete structure consisting of the pier as well as its footing.

Frost line. The lowest depth at which the ground will freeze. It determines the code-required depth for footings.

Girder. See Beam.

Grade. The top surface of the ground. Grading also refers to the act of excavating, leveling, and compacting dirt to its desired finished level.

Header joist. A joist attached across the ends of field joists that supports them. Sometimes attached to the house and called a ledger.

Hot-dipped galvanized (HDG) nails. Nails dipped in zinc rather than electroplated. Superior for outdoor construction.

Joist. 2-by lumber, set on edge, that supports decking. It is supported by beams, ledgers, or header joists.

Joist hanger. Metal connecting device for attaching a joist at right angles to a ledger or header joist so their top edges are flush.

KDAT (Kiln Dried After Treatment). Pressure-treated lumber that is more expensive than untreated lumber but much less likely to warp.

Lag screw or bolt. Heavy-duty screw with a bolt head for attaching structural members to a wall or to material too thick for a machine bolt to go through.

Layout. The process of marking points on the ground for accurate placement of footings and posts. Also refers to marking boards at the points where other boards will be attached.

Ledger. A 2-by or wider piece of lumber bolted to the house for supporting the ends of joists. Technically refers only to a board placed under the joist ends, but often refers to any member bolted to the house. See Header joist.

Loads. The weights and forces any structure is designed to counteract, such as dead loads (the structure itself) and live loads (all potential occupants and furnishings, snow load, wind uplift, and earthquake forces).

Pier. A small concrete or masonry structure that holds a post off the ground. It has its own footing and can be precast or cast in place.

Plumb. Perfectly vertical.

Post. A vertical support, either resting on a pier or buried directly in the ground, that holds up a deck. Also refers to a vertical railing support.

Preservative. Chemical substance applied to wood for resisting decay and insects. Most types are available only to licensed applicators or manufacturers of pressure-treated lumber.

Pressure treatment. A process of forcing preservatives into wood. One commonly used waterborne preservative is chromated copper arsenate (CCA), specified for aboveground (LP-2) or ground-contact (LP-22) use. Depending on the chemical used, the wood will have a greenish or brownish tint.

Rail. Horizontal railing member.

Reinforcing bar. Steel rods for reinforcing concrete.

Rim joist. See Band joist.

Riser. In stair construction, the vertical dimension or "rise" of any step.

Screening. The maximum opening allowed between railing members. The distance varies by code (typically 6 inches or 9 inches).

Site. The location for a structure or improvement.

Sleeper. A horizontal wood member laid directly on ground, patio, or roof for supporting a deck.

Slope. Ground with an inclined surface, usually measured as a percentage (units of vertical rise per 100 units of horizontal distance).

Spacing. The distance between repetitive members, measured "on center" (center to center).

Span. The distance between supports, measured center to center.

Spindle. Small-dimensioned baluster.

Stair stringers. The heavy, inclined members that support a stairway's treads. Can be solid, with treads attached between the stringers, or cut out, with treads resting on top of the sawtooth sections. Also called carriages.

Stringer. A main bearing member that acts like a beam but is only 2-by lumber bolted to the sides of posts. See also Stair stringers.

Tread. The horizontal dimension of each step in a stairway. Also the step itself.

Zinc-coated. Protected by a shiny metallic coating for outdoor use. Refers to nails and hardware. See Corrosion-resistant connectors.

Zoning requirements. Local ordinances that may affect a deck's size or location, such as setback limits (minimum distance from the property line to the structure), lot coverage (maximum percentage of the lot that can be covered by all improvements), and even the deck's size or height.

INDEX

U.S. Measure and Metric Measure Conversion Chart

	Symbol	Formulas for Exact Measures			Rounded Measures for Quick Reference		
		When you know:	Multiply by	To find:			
Mass (Weight)	oz	ounces	28.35	grams	1 oz		= 30 g
	lb	pounds	0.45	kilograms	4 oz		= 115 g
	g	grams	0.035	ounces	8 oz		= 225 g
	kg	kilograms	2.2	pounds	16 oz	= 1 lb	= 450 kg
					32 oz	= 2 lb	= 900 kg
					36 oz	= 2 1/4 lb	= 1000g (a kg)
Volume	tsp	teaspoons	5.0	milliliters	1/4 tsp	= 1/24 oz	= 1 ml
	tbsp	tablespoons	15.0	milliliters	1/2 tsp	= 1/12 oz	= 2 ml
	fl oz	fluid ounces	29.57	milliliters	1 tsp	= 1/6 oz	= 5 ml
	c	cups	0.24	liters	1 tbsp	= 1/2 oz	= 15 ml
	pt	pints	0.47	liters	1 c	= 8 oz	= 250 ml
	qt	quarts	0.95	liters	2 c (1 pt)	= 16 oz	= 500 ml
	gal	gallons	3.785	liters	4 c (1 qt)	= 32 oz	= 1 l
	ml	milliliters	0.034	fluid ounces	4 qt (1 gal)	= 128 oz	= 3 3/4-l
Length	in.	inches	2.54	centimeters	3/8 in.		= 1 cm
	ft	feet	30.48	centimeters	1 in.		= 2.5 cm
	yd	yards	0.9144	meters	2 in.		= 5 cm
	mi	miles	1.609	kilometers	2-1/2 in.		= 6.5 cm
	km	kilometers	0.621	miles	12 in. (1 ft)		= 30 cm
	m	meters	1.094	yards	1 yd		= 90 cm
	cm	centimeters	0.39	inches	100 ft		= 30 m
					1 mi		= 1.6 km
Temperature	°F	Fahrenheit	5/9 (after subtracting 32)	Celsius	32°F		= 0°C
					68°F		= 20°C
	°C	Celsius	9/5 (then add 32)	Fahrenheit	212°F		= 100°C
Area	in.²	square inches	6.452	square centimeters	1 in.²		= 6.5 cm²
	ft²	square feet	929.0	square centimeters	1 ft²		= 930 cm²
	yd²	square yards	8361.0	square centimeters	1 yd²		= 8360 cm²
	a	acres	0.4047	hectares	1 a		= 4050 m²